Lincoln Christian College

W9-BRR-051

THE
TIME
IT IS

A Play about Jesus

Dan Otto Via

UNIVERSITY
PRESS OF
AMERICA

© 1982 by **Dan Otto Via**

University Press of America, Inc.

P.O. Box 19101, Washington, D.C. 20036

All rights reserved

Printed in the United States of America

ISBN (Perfect): 0-8191-2484-2
ISBN (Cloth): 0-8191-2483-4

This work is subject to royalty. For any reading or performance by amateur or professional on stage, television, film, or by any other medium, permission must be secured.

Library of Congress Catalog Card Number: **82-45056**

FOR

DANNY AND CARTER

67172

iii

ACKNOWLEDGMENTS

When the dialogue contains direct biblical quotations, they come from the Revised Standard Version of the Bible, copyrighted 1946, 1952 © 1971, 1973.

To the University of Virginia goes my gratitude for a grant to prepare the manuscript. And for reading the play in helpfully critical ways, I should like to express my thanks to several good friends--Bob Alley, Neva and Julian Hartt, Dick Myers, and Nathan Scott. I am also very grateful to Shirley and Howard Strobel for long reading, listening and talking sessions at Wintergreen during autumn weekends in two successive years. My wife and family were supportive, as they have always been, and listened to my reading more times than they should have had to. They usually responded as I hoped they would. It is to my two sons that the play is dedicated.

Dan Otto Via

Charlottesville, Virginia
February, 1982

CHARACTERS

Chara
Jesus
First worker
Second worker
Vineyard owner
Overseer
Third worker
James, the brother of Jesus
James, the disciple
Peter
John
Andrew
First would-be follower
Second would-be follower
Friend of the paralytic
Another friend of the
   paralytic
Paralytic
Asa the scribe
Man in the crowd
Levi
Demoniac
Woman with hemorrhage
Bartholomew
Nazareth townsman
Second Nazareth townsman
Messenger
Wedding guest
Host
Servant
Second guest
Third guest
Bystander
Second bystander
Woman from Phoenicia
Man in the crowd
Another man
Well dressed man

Priest
Centurion
Caiaphas
Priest
Second priest
High priest's maid
Bystander
Pilate
Priest
Soldier
Second soldier
Third soldier
Priest
Second priest
Third priest
Joy
Bart
Paul
Mark

ACT I

Antioch

A Question

The cooling breeze from the Mediterranean which blows up the Orontes toward Syrian Antioch makes the long, hot summer in the city bearable. It no doubt comes as a surprise to twentieth century moderns to discover that the ancient founders of Antioch, having set the city between the river and Mount Sulpius, then laid out the main streets so as to take advantage of the breeze and the shade. An early first century traveler walking upstream from the sea, following the breeze, just before arriving at the great city would find himself in Daphne. The splendid suburb has a wealth of villas and baths. Food, drink, and entertainment are plentifully available in its colonnades and restaurants--in one of which, a small outdoor place, on a bright sunlit afternoon, sit a young man and woman--a boy and a girl--talking. A loaf of bread and pitcher of wine are on the table, and they are eating.

                    CHARA
Your name is Jesus and you're from Galilee--you said Nazareth?

                    JESUS
Yes, that's right. Here, have some wine.

He pours wine into both of their cups and they drink some slowly.

                    CHARA
And what has brought you to the fair crown of the Orient, Tyche's city?

                    JESUS
Is that what you call Antioch?

                    CHARA
That's what they call it. I don't know that I would. But you haven't told me why you came here.

                    JESUS
Perhaps I didn't know it when I came, but-- well, I came in the hope of gaining good fortune from the goddess, from Tyche.

CHARA

You don't talk like a Jew. And you speak
Greek.

JESUS

Lots of people speak Greek in Galilee. It's
not that hard. Perhaps my reasons for coming
here, for leaving home, were not very Jewish.
But then, again, they were. Let's just say I
wanted to take a journey to a far country.
Have you always lived here, Chara?

CHARA

No, my family moved here a few years ago from
the south, from Phoenicia, near Tyre. It's not
far from Galilee, you know.

JESUS

I do know. We were almost neighbors--if we
weren't of different religions. I suppose I
really shouldn't be sitting here at this table
with you.

CHARA

Why in the world not?

JESUS

Why?

CHARA

Oh, yes, your jealous Jewish god, the Lord,
I've heard of him. You are to worship him and
only him--and not associate with the likes of
us gentiles.

JESUS

I know it sounds severe, intolerant, irra-
tional. But I **am** trying to serve him--though
he makes things difficult for me.

CHARA

Really. I'm sure. But what kind of diffi-
culties--exactly?

JESUS

I don't know what he wants with me, or with
Israel. That's why I left home in part. I'm
trying to understand what God proposes, and I'm

spending my father's money. He's a good man, less religious than some. But my brother, James--he loves the law, studies it constantly, wants to obey it in every detail, and wants everyone else to.

CHARA

You're not all that devoted to the law?

JESUS

I respect the law. How could I not? It makes me feel responsible and makes the world hold together. It tells Israel that if she is righteous she will prosper. But where is our prosperity? Are we so unrighteous? Should I listen to the writings that say the world gets worse all the time and will end soon? And then there are the prophets. They make even greater demands on us and also promise disaster if we fail. But they promise renewal as well. Where does God speak? He is somehow present in my family, and in Nazareth, but something there oppresses me. I suppose I left home and God-- to find God. And I suppose I must be boring you.

CHARA

No, Jesus, you're not actually. It will surprise you--me being a pagan and all--but I'm interested in religion. I've spent a lot of time in temples and shrines. I have stood on the fringes of the philosophers' halls. I've thought, and I've felt. Sometimes I feel I belong to the world, but often-- more often?--I don't know--I feel I don't. The ground I walk on, the grape, the olive trees, the beautiful colonnades built through the heart of Antioch, other people--they seem so alien. My own body- -is it wicked? Is it **mine**? Everything is unreal.

JESUS

My god, you're more pessimistic than the preachers of doom in Galilee. What about Tyche, good fortune? Doesn't Antioch belong to her?

CHARA

I don't believe in her. I said that, didn't I?

5

JESUS

Maybe you did, Chara. I'm not sure. I didn't
hear it. Well.... who do you believe in? I
don't know much about Greek or Syrian deities,
but I've heard of some of them. Is it
Cybele....or Astarte?

CHARA

No! Haven't you heard their myths? They're
too dangerous--

She smiles at him, gently, if teasingly.

CHARA (cont.)

--for men. But you've got to have some role in
this unreal world, something to get you out of
it, so I have chosen Isis. I've been ini-
tiated, and reborn as the goddess.

She stands up and looks at him with momentary imperi-
ousness and then resumes with obvious mock-seriousness.

CHARA (cont.)

I am **I s i s.**

And she smiles at him teasingly, if not gently.

CHARA (cont.)

--or her priestess--or her prostitute.

Shock and disappointment register briefly on Jesus'
face. Then he laughs freely and without holding back,
less intense than he has been thus far.

JESUS

Chara, you're priceless. I don't know exactly
what you mean by that. I'll have to find out--
probably more and less than it sounds like.
But there's a sense in which it couldn't be
more appropriate. Because I can just hear my
brother James talking to my father now.
"Father," he will say. "Father, Jesus is off
devouring your living with harlots."

CHARA

Is James your older brother?

JESUS

No, I'm the oldest in the family. But somehow
James seems to be the steadiest.

6

CHARA

Yes, you will have to find out what I meant, but I've got to go home. My mother will expect me to help her with the evening meal.

JESUS

And I've got to find work soon. My money's running out....I hope I'll see you again. Could you meet me here a week from today, in the afternoon?

CHARA

I could. I will. Good-by.

JESUS

(smiling)

Good-by.

2.

In a vineyard on a hillside sloping toward the mountain, just beyond the wall of Antioch, a number of workers are picking grapes. It is late in the day, and two or three workers are talking together.

JESUS

God, it's hot! Where the hell is Antioch's celebrated breeze?

FIRST WORKER

It's late today, usually begins about noon. But we may still have a cool evening.

JESUS

I hope so. I've worked since early morning in this sun. A cup of wine in a cool spot tonight would be good.

SECOND WORKER

I hadn't seen you before today. You don't live in Antioch, do you?

JESUS

No, I'm from Galilee. But I've been here for a while. I've found a place to stay in the Jewish quarter, and I'm trying to find out what's going on in the city.

FIRST WORKER

A lot. You'll see. How did you happen to get a job with a Jewish vineyard owner?

JESUS

By chance, pure chance. I went down to the market early this morning to look for work, and he came along and hired me. I've put in a long day for my denarius, but it's almost over.

FIRST WORKER

The boss is **strange**. Have you seen the way he's been hiring people all day long?

SECOND WORKER

I've seen it. Some of these fellows have only worked an hour. You might think he would have noticed this morning how much work there was to do.

JESUS

Well, they certainly won't be getting much money. How many ways can you divide a denarius? It hardly seems worth their effort.

The owner and his overseer appear on the scene.

OVERSEER
(loudly to the whole group of workers)

Day's end! Quitting time! If you'll all come here, I'll pay you your wages.

All the workers gather around the two men.

OWNER
(to the overseer but in the hearing of all)

Pay each one of them a denarius.

The overseer begins to hand out the coins and is completing the job as the first man to be paid speaks.

THIRD WORKER
(to the owner in wondering amazement and obvious gratitude)

Sir, I only worked....I hadn't expected.... Thank you.
(to himself as he walks off)
We can eat tonight.

JESUS
(to the owner)

Sir, some of these men worked just part of the

day or even only an hour, but you've made them
equal to those of us who've borne the scorch-
ing heat of the whole day.

                    OWNER
Friend, I'm doing you no wrong. You agreed to
work for a denarius. It's the customary wage.
Why do you resent my generosity to those who
worked less? Can I not do what I choose with
my own money?

                    JESUS
I suppose you can, but not to commit injustice. Unfairness has got no right to parade
itself as generosity. We've worked hard--some
of us--we haven't been strolling around
watching the others. Look at all of the
grapes we've picked. If you wanted to pay
those who worked an hour a denarius, you had
the right, but then you should've paid us
more. A day's worth more than an hour.
That's simple justice, it's not hard to see.
There's justice, and there's injustice.
That's all there is.

                    OWNER
And you can't see any other possibility.

                    JESUS
No, there isn't any!

                    OWNER
You have your denarius. Take what's yours--
and go.

                       3.

    Jesus is standing in front of the outdoor res-
taurant in Daphne when Chara walks up to him. Spon-
taneously and unexpectedly they touch hands, briefly
and shyly. Together they walk to a table and sit
down.

                    JESUS
How's the week gone?

                    CHARA
Not bad. I'm glad you were here. I thought
maybe you wouldn't be.

9

JESUS

Why would I not be? I said I would, that is, I asked you to meet me.

CHARA

Oh, you would have had your reasons. You were looking for work you might not find, you were running out of money, you are in a foreign country you might not like.

JESUS

I found work--it lasted a day, and I haven't found any more. I picked grapes for a vineyard owner who admittedly paid me a fair day's wage, but then the crazy man gave a denarius to other people--some of them had hardly worked an hour. I confronted him with his injustice, and he fired me. A man works an hour and is treated as if he'd worked a day. Who can put up with that kind of stuff? It's as absurd as saying the first are last and the last are first.

CHARA

Hey, Jesus, wait a minute. You're losing me. I thought it was your brother James who was so devoted to the law   and you raised the questions. But you've got quite a mind for exact justice yourself.

JESUS
(with restrained surprise)

It appears I have. I guess I didn't quite know it. I thought I was so free. I could break with convention, leave home, ask my father for money he couldn't really spare, transgress what was expected of me, if not the law. But when my own work was on the line, I wanted the assurance of justice. You do it right, you are rewarded. I suppose I am threatened by what can't be calculated. And I shouldn't be. Even Moses taught us better, not to mention the prophets. Why did God choose Israel, why are we the holy people? Not because we were righteous, but because others were worse. Not because we were important, but because for some never clarified reason he chose to love us.

CHARA

Then there is something in your own religion other than clear justice or injustice.

10

                         JESUS
No, there isn't.

                         CHARA
But you have just said there is-- "We were not
chosen because we were righteous."

                         JESUS
I take it back.

                         CHARA
Jesus, wouldn't you sometimes like to receive
unexpected and undeserved generosity?

                         JESUS
How did we get on to religion anyway?   We were
talking about my getting fired.

                         CHARA
Maybe there's a connection.

                         JESUS
Maybe there is, but it would take a prophet to
see it. You said you were a priestess of Isis.
Maybe you're a prophet of the Lord, too.
(ironically)

                         CHARA
Hardly, I'm a pagan. Remember? But in my pur-
suit of religions I have spent some time at the
synagogue. You know, all the other religions
just sort of slide right into each other. But
Judaism won't fit. It intrigues me--at a distance, but I can't figure it out. And you, my
Jewish   friend,   are   evading   my   question.
Wouldn't you--to use your terms--like to be the
last who is made first?

                         JESUS
No, I would **not**.   I don't want what I don't
deserve.

                         CHARA
What did you deserve for leaving home?

                         JESUS
And you're also handy with the knife. I had my
reasons.

                           11

CHARA

Reasons your family would recognize?

JESUS

I don't know.....I don't know, but I will make it right.

CHARA

Just suppose that day in the vineyard you **were** one of the ones who got more than he worked for.

JESUS

I wouldn't have wanted it.

CHARA

Suppose you desperately needed it, and suppose you could not **not** need it.... Maybe that's where the gods come in. They give us what we can't help needing--or wanting.

JESUS

If that's the case, something will have to change in me. Maybe I have some things to sort out. But you seem to have composed your life very smoothly--you and Isis. Or I guess it can't be you **and** Isis--
          (mockingly but not sarcastically)
since you **are** Isis.

CHARA

No, the composition of my life always threatens to dissolve. That's why I need and serve the goddess.

JESUS

But you don't really need her. You do quite well on your own.

CHARA

I do need her. She gives me immortality. I don't want my soul to fall into nothing when I die or suffer in the underworld--and it won't. I will be completely united with Isis.

JESUS

What about this life?

CHARA

She helps me here, too. Isis dwells in highest
heaven with the original Forefather, so she's
above the deities of the lower heavens and the
gods of this world, the star gods. They're the
ones we need deliverance from. They made this
world in the first place--which was a terrible
mistake. And now they want to rule our lives
and keep us from highest heaven. They're fate.
But being reborn as Isis lifts me above all of
that.

JESUS

How does Isis get in touch with you, Chara?
Did she have prophets? Has she given her word
in Scriptures?

CHARA

Oh, we have our myths, beautiful stories about
what the gods and goddesses have done, and the
priests interpret them, and some philosophers,
too, in a way. But the rites are the important
thing. That's how we really make contact.

JESUS

What are they? What do you do?

CHARA

Oh, there're quite a few things we can do. You
can go down and wash yourself in the salt water
of the sea. A meal of communion is good.
Or....you can sprinkle on a little pig's blood.
But the most effective rite of all, Jesus, ah,
the best of all--is making love.

JESUS

Sometimes I don't know what you're serious
about. You can talk about how you see life and
the world and your religion with unmixed ear-
nestness, and then you can mention the rites as
if they're a joke.

CHARA

Yes, I can do that. But, Jesus, even religion
deserves a measure of detachment.   I am,
however, serious about making love.

JESUS
(hesitatingly)
Chara, are you really a prostitute?

13

                         CHARA
                (smiling with warm affection)
No, Jesus, not in the ordinary sense, not in
any commercial sense.   I was partly teasing
you, but I am looking for Osiris to love.   My
whole life in a way is a ritual.   I'm acting
out Isis' search for Osiris. Her search is my
role, my way of dealing with a misbegotten
world.   I want to restore Osiris' fragmented
body and love him--or I want to love his
fragments back together.   Will you be my
Osiris, Jesus? I need you so I can be Isis. I
want you.

                         JESUS
                (looks around, looks at her)
You stir me, Chara, but that's both too much
reason and not enough reason for wanting me. I
can't be Osiris.   It's my very best hope that
I'll be Jesus. But now you're puzzling me.   It
seems to me you've almost been saying the body
is evil.   So how can love in the body unite you
with Isis--or Osiris?

                         CHARA
It's simple, it really is simple.   Our bodies
desire connection with another body.   And our
souls--or   spirits--or   whatever,   which   are
divine themselves, desire union with the gods.

                         JESUS
But I still don't see how human, bodily love
has anything to do with your quest for divi-
nity.   You've made body and soul almost ene-
mies.

                         CHARA
Well, maybe almost but not quite.   Perhaps....
perhaps the union of our bodies would somehow
help out the union of our spirits with each
other, and with the gods.

                         JESUS
I accept the goodness of the body, Chara.   I
really do.   How could I look at you and not?
The Scriptures of my faith even teach me to
accept it.   But the law says love belongs in
marriage.

                          14

CHARA

Oh, yes, the law of your stingy god! What does he **not** want to withhold? He is one of the gods of this world, and he wants to enslave us with his laws. But the original Forefather doesn't care what we do with our bodies. Isis doesn't care. In fact, we ought to break the law of your god to show we belong to highest heaven, to show we are free of this world.

JESUS

I know I said "the law says," but it really isn't a matter of law, Chara. It's not for-bidding for the sake of forbidding, requiring obedience for the sake of obedience. The Lord doesn't withhold what is good because he's stingy. It's a matter of how we are made, of what we are.

CHARA

I don't know what to make of you, Jesus, you and your strange god, but you do charm me, and I've talked to you late into the afternoon, I must go.

JESUS

Meet me here next week?

CHARA

No (pauses, and laughs), but come to the Daphne Gate about an hour later than this, and I'll take you to one of our family's olive groves and we can watch the sun set.

JESUS

Chara, how can you say the world is a terrible mistake and also want to see the sun go down in the Orontes Valley--with me?

CHARA

I don't know....but I do. I **am** looking for Osiris, but I like you, too, Jesus.

JESUS

And I, you. I'll be there.... I trust I'll be there, I have to find work this week. But whatever happens, I'll see you.

15

I'll see you.

4.

On a farm outside Antioch Jesus is in the field talking with another worker. A fence stands nearby with pigs grazing on the other side of it.

WORKER
Are you still complaining about the heat?

JESUS
I would be--if I had the energy to complain. But why do you ask?

WORKER
You were complaining about it last week when we were picking grapes together.

JESUS
So we were. I'm sorry I didn't recognize you. I've had a lot of things on my mind.

WORKER
Evidently. Are things really going as bad for you as you say?

JESUS
Pretty bad. This morning I was out of money, out of food, and out of friends.... Well, there's one friend, a kind of friend. And here I am in the only job I could find, working for a gentile, feeding the pigs no less.

WORKER
That would be hard on a Jewish boy fresh out of Palestine. What happened to your money?

JESUS
Well, you have to eat. You have to have a place to sleep. And if you come to a far country to learn about the strangeness of the place, you've got to spend some time looking-- even if your Jewishness clings a lot closer to you than you'd thought.

                    WORKER
And yours clings.

                    JESUS
In some kind of way, yes.

                    WORKER
Why don't you go home?

                    JESUS
I've thought about it--very intently. I left
home to find freedom--and find God, but I think
I'm going to have to find those things in
Israel. And then there's the prompting of the
carob pods.

                    WORKER
              (not getting the point)
The carob pods? What do they have to do with
it?

                    JESUS
If nothing else they remind me of the despera-
tion of my sheer physical hunger. Carob pods
are pigs' food, and what is more unclean than a
pig? Yet I would eat their food if the boss
would give me some. But there's also the other
part. One of our rabbis said, "When Israel has
been reduced to eating carob pods she's ready
to return." Well, I've been reduced, so maybe
I should consider returning.

                    WORKER
And what are you going to find at home?

                    JESUS
Something better, I think, than I've found in
Antioch, though one thing I've found here holds
me, holds me and perplexes me. But I've got to
come to terms with my life in Galilee. I can
work there. My father's carpentry shop is
modestly prosperous. He even employs a couple
of hired hands in addition to the family.
There is love also in Nazareth. My mother's
love is almost too clutching. My father's is
different. Sometimes when we're working
together, I see him looking at me as if across
a distance neither of us understands while in

his eyes there's a tenderness you don't expect
from a father.

                    WORKER
So the wandering son **is** going to return?

                    JESUS
Not quite, not the wandering **son**. I've for-
feited the right to be a son. I wouldn't want
it. I don't think I could handle it. What
there's left for me to do is to pick myself up
and go back and say "Father, I've sinned
against you and against God. I'm not worthy to
be your son, but would you let me work as one
of your hired hands?"

                    5.

    Jesus and Chara having met at the Daphne Gate,
arrive at the olive grove, holding hands. They sit
down.

                    CHARA
But, Jesus, I do not understand why you have to
go back home.

                    JESUS
Because, I've tried to tell you, that's where I
have to find out if God is saying something
specifically to me. Is he calling me to do
something, some special thing? At times I
think maybe he is--but it's so ridiculous. Why
me, when there are so many reasons that make it
improbable? And what would I do--or be? The
rabbis often get stranded in the details of the
law. That doesn't seem promising. The
prophets have long since ceased to speak in
Israel. What--?

                    CHARA
But why do you have to go back to Galilee?
Surely your god is present also in Antioch.
There are plenty of Jews here for you to talk
to. And I'm here, Jesus, I'm here.

                    JESUS
I know you're here, and that's the one thing

18

that makes it hard for me to leave. But I have
to.   It was in Palestine that our history has
taken place and the Lord has been involved with
us.   That's where the law was given and the
prophets spoke.   I have to find my connection
with all of that.   In fact, I have to find out
how a pig can **have** a connection with all of
that.

                    CHARA
A pig?

                    JESUS
Yes, me. I told you I would have eaten pigs'
fodder. If you eat with someone--or something--
you become one of them.   I would have, so I'm a
pig (angrily, self-accusingly, but then
laughing). Should I not say--"Oink, oink?"

                    CHARA
Jesus, you're not a pig (laughing, but then
serious). Don't leave now. Don't leave me. I
love you.

                    JESUS
Do you love **me**--or the possibility I might be
Osiris?

                    CHARA
          (pausing, thinking)
Both...but I do **love** you.

                    JESUS
And I love you.

He gently pushes her back to the ground and kisses
her, not briefly, and warmly. And she responds.

                    JESUS (cont.)
Your lips distil nectar, my love.   Honey and
milk are under your tongue.

                    CHARA
Ah, Jesus. Your kisses aren't the only beautiful thing that comes from your lips. Where did
you get those words?

                    JESUS
Well, I could have got them from my imagina-

tion--and from you. I have an imagination, you
know, and you are certainly powerful enough to
bring it to life. In a sense that's where I
did get them. But more directly I got them
from a poem, a poem in the word of my strange
God.

                    CHARA
Jesus, look at the color the sun's left in the
sky. Look at the mountains. Look at the olive
trees. Look at me.... Make love to me.

                    JESUS
I couldn't tell you how much I want to, how
much I desire you, but I can not.

                    CHARA
Because of the law, it's forbidden by the law?
Surely not here, not now, not when we love each
other, not when we're never going to see each
other again.

                    JESUS
Chara, please don't pull me apart. How can I
make you understand? It's not because it's for-
bidden by the law. God, I feel ridiculous.
You want to make love and so do I, but instead
I give you a speech about what it means. But
I want you to understand. You once asked if
your body is really yours.

                    CHARA
I know now it is mine.

                    JESUS
                (smiles)
But it's much more than **yours**. It's **you**, but
just you. I know we don't agree on this, but I
don't think God is **in** me--or in you.

                    CHARA
I thought you Jews were the religious ones, but
it seems it's us.

                    JESUS
We are religious in **our** way. God is not in us,
but he makes us alive and gives us ourselves
and the world to live in. God scooped up some

dirt and breathed life into it, and the result
was a living soul. I don't think my soul is a
part of God sadly imprisoned in my wicked body.
My soul **is** my living body. We're not in two
parts, but one. We're whole people--or we
should be.

                    CHARA
That's so strange to me, Jesus. You don't know
how strange it sounds. I can't really take it
in, but it does somehow speak to things I feel
at   times....As   I   think   of   it   (smiling
brightly), it ought to make love-making even
better--if we're all that much in our bodies.

                    JESUS
I think it would make it better. It makes it
go further, and it makes it ask more of us. If
my soul is my living body, my flesh is my soul.
When a man and a woman make love they become
one flesh, so one soul. Chara, if I tell you I
love you with my flesh, I have committed it
all, said all there is to say, offered all I
can offer. I don't believe I can do that and
leave you tomorrow.

                    CHARA
            (with tears, touching his face)
I almost think I understand you, but I'll never
see you again.

                    JESUS
Maybe so--sometime, somewhere.

Jesus stands up and takes her by the hand, helping her
up. They look into each others eyes.

                    JESUS (cont.)
I think we've said good-by without having
actually said the words. I'm glad of that.

                    CHARA
Yes.

They kiss, holding each other, lingering.

                    JESUS
Chara, you are my joy.

                        21

CHARA

Jesus, you are my love.

6.

A few years later in the small courtyard of their home in Nazareth in Galilee Jesus and James are talking.

JAMES

So, Jesus, you're going to take to the streets, the roads, the seaside--to preach. Isn't this rather sudden?

JESUS

Yes and no. I've been feeling the press of something like this for a long time. Remember, Jeremiah felt the word of God was a burning fire in his heart that wouldn't let him keep silent. It's been like that, but I've just decided to do it.

JAMES

Why now?

JESUS

Well, you know I was baptized by John the Baptist. I think that's what finally made my decision for me.

JAMES

Are you going to continue John's message--the wrath of God is about to destroy us, the ax is laid to the root of the tree, the end is at hand?

JESUS

Now how about that, James? I'm glad John's message is so well known. Yes, I'll preach that. I feel a great urgency about the nearness of God's reign.

JAMES

That's crazy, Jesus. These preachers of doom and destruction are mad men. God has promised peace and well-being and long life in the land to a righteous and obedient Israel.

JESUS

So we live under Rome. Is that such a holiday?
And what kind of obedience has Israel given?
Time is running out.

JAMES

Jesus, if you've got to have a mission, then be
a rabbi.   You already know more about the
Scriptures than most of the rabbis, and God
knows you've spent enough time with them.
Continue your study of the law and be a
teacher.

JESUS

I don't think I could quite fit into that. I
find too many things in the prophets and other
writings that raise questions about the law for
me.   I even sometimes find the law speaking
against itself.

JAMES

What about our family?   Don't you feel any
responsibility for it?   After all, you're the
oldest.   Father is dead.   Mother has to be
cared for, and we still have an unmarried
brother and sister. You've been a good worker
in our shop, Jesus. People respect you and we
need you.   It would be difficult to get along
without you.

JESUS

I can understand that, James, and it gives me
no little pain.   That's one reason why it's
taken me so long to make my decision. But it's
made, and I have to go.

JAMES

Just exactly what do you see yourself as doing?
Are you a prophet?   Are you resurrecting
prophecy, the living word of God, after these
centuries of silence?

JESUS

I'm not too sure about what my status is.
That's a question I'm still pursuing, but I do
know I have a message to proclaim.

JAMES

But why you Jesus?   If the message is that

important why would it be given to you--I mean
why would it be given to you or to me, or to
anyone we know? You were baptized by John.
Doesn't he preach a baptism of repentance for
the forgiveness of sins--which you apparently
thought you needed? Is the one who needs
repentance and forgiveness going to call on
others to repent?

                    JESUS
Who else would there be to do it?

                    JAMES
            (ignoring the last remark)
And remember your little trip to Antioch a few
years back. You left home, wasted the family's
money, consorted with gentiles, frequented
wineshops--and who knows what else.

                    JESUS
I'll shock you a little more, James. I just
told you I don't know exactly what role God has
called me to, but at the moment of my baptism
powerful things--perplexing things--were strug-
gling in my heart. I seemed to hear the word
of the Lord to the king: "You are my son,
today I have begotten you. Ask of me, and I
will make the nations your heritage." And then
I heard the word of the prophet: "Behold my
servant, my chosen one, in whom my soul
delights." That's God's servant, Israel, who
will be despised and rejected in bringing his
reign to all the gentiles. How can I be the
royal son of God? How can I be the suffering
Israel?

                    JAMES
You're asking me? I was only asking you how
you could be a preacher of repentance.

                    JESUS
Yes, how can I? I went to Antioch, left home,
to find God. But God has found me--in ways I
couldn't have anticipated. And that's given me
a message.

                    JAMES
How has he found you, Jesus?

67172

JESUS

In a number of ways. You referred to my little
trip to Antioch. I hung out in the outdoor
restaurants--and who knows what else. Well,
there was a girl.

JAMES

A gentile, I suppose.

JESUS

Yes indeed.

JAMES

And I suppose you slept with her. That's the
gentile way.

JESUS

No, I didn't sleep with her. But perhaps I
should have. In any case, she asked me some
hard questions. She made me think about God,
myself, the world around me, as I hadn't
before.

JAMES

You were instructed about God by a gentile
girl?

JESUS

That's not so absurd. The Lord, holy as he is,
seems to work in very human ways. The world
gets taken up into his word. The prophets
speak of him very poetically. They bring God
and the world together.

JAMES

You're obsessed with the prophets.

JESUS

Maybe I am. But how do they tell us God acts?
He will shave the haughty nations like a
razor. He planted with love a choice vineyard
--us--but we only yielded wild grapes. So the
vineyard has got to come down. What's the Lord
like? Why he's like a moth, an ulcer, dry rot
eating away at Israel. And you know the
prophet Ezekiel, Ezekiel the wild man. Remember
what he said the Lord did to disobedient
Israel? He gave us bad laws, laws that take

25

Lincoln Christian College

away life, laws that make us offer him our children as sacrifices--to horrify us.

                    JAMES
Jesus, you've got an exaggerated talent for locating the most offensive things in the Scriptures. I didn't even know they were there. I'm not sure they are there!

                    JESUS
They're there all right. I suppose we have to question what they mean for us, but I expect that at some point in being found by God we have to be offended. And then there is hope after the razor and dry rot have finished their work. The Lord is going to give us a new heart, a softened heart, a new covenant with him.

                    JAMES
He'll give it to us when we've become obedient, when we've returned to him. Moses has taught us that if we obey the commandments we will have life and possess the land.

                    JESUS
I hope he gives us life before we become obedient. Otherwise we may never have it.

                    JAMES
Why not?

                    JESUS
Because we're not able to be obedient. We don't know the Lord because the **spirit** of harlotry has taken hold of us. We can't return to the Lord because the power of our acts doesn't permit us to return. So he has to come after us. Hosea went looking for his wife while she was still an adulteress. And the Lord comes looking for us while we're still pursuing strange gods.

                    JAMES
Jesus, in the heat of argument I have lost sight of something important--we love you. Isn't that what it means to be an Israelite? Under God, under the law, we love each other

and care for each other in the family, and in the community. Love holds the community together. Don't leave home and do something foolish.

JESUS

I have to leave the family, James, so I can belong to it in a different way. And really there's a sense in which the family has become incomparably important to me. You asked how God found me. Well, he found me when my father welcomed me back from Antioch as a son, without even giving me a chance to make my confession. He couldn't afford a fatted calf or a ring or a fine robe, but there was no doubt that I was his son and not a hired hand--when I might not even be his son and certainly hadn't been behaving like it.

JAMES
(shocked)

You know you're our father's son. You know you're Joseph's son. There couldn't be such a thing in our family. Our mother....our father....Surely not.

JESUS

James, you needn't deceive yourself or try to protect me. Maybe you're right. It's always been uncertain. But do they call me the son of Mary for nothing? That, however, isn't too important. Whatever the facts may have been, I could not have been any more genuinely loved than I was by Joseph. And that's given me something to proclaim.

JAMES

If you're going to be a prophet, Jesus, or whatever it is you're going to do, I would think you would have been given a vision or a sign. But it seems that all you've done is read the Scriptures, and look around at the world, and somehow you've got a message.

JESUS

Well, maybe that's how it happens, but the message does have me. Years ago I believed I didn't want what I didn't deserve. But when I returned home not deserving to be my father's son and being a son again was nevertheless offered to me, I discovered I did want it. Because I also discovered that the power of the gift overtakes the shock to your pride--the shock that occurs when you accept the gift undeserved.

                    JAMES
And it **was** thoroughly undeserved.

                    JESUS
Yes, it was. But Hosea loved his adulterous wife, and Joseph loved his wayward son. Now I've got to do whatever it takes to show Israel my father in heaven is as good as my father on earth.

ACT II

Galilee

A Questioning Affirmation

Two weeks later Jesus has moved to Capernaum by the Sea of Galilee and one day shortly thereafter is beside the sea preaching to twenty or thirty people. Within earshot four young fishermen, two pairs of brothers, are repairing a boat. Close-by an older man and three helpers are sitting beside another boat working on a net. As Jesus gets into his sermon, the four fishermen stop their work and begin to listen to him.

                    JESUS
The time the prophets proclaimed is now ful-
filled, the reign of God is at hand--but you
won't believe it. You'll be eating and
drinking, marrying and giving in marriage, and
generally raising hell. Everything is per-
fectly normal, as it was in the days of Noah--
until the flood struck--very unexpectedly.
That time is coming and that time is here.
That time gives us everything and that time
asks everything of us. The Lord has anointed
me to preach good news to the poor, release to
the captives, recovery of sight to the blind,
liberty to the oppressed, forgiveness to sinners. Repent, turn yourselves around, and
believe this good news. God is about to end
this age and bring in his marvelous new time.
I am here to announce your last chance.

When Jesus finishes speaking, the crowd disperses with people giving each other wondering glances. Jesus walks over to the four fishermen, followed at a short distance by several men who listen in on his conver-sation.

                    JESUS
Did you hear what I was saying?

                    JAMES
We couldn't get away from it.

                    JESUS
What are your names anyway?

                    PETER
My name is Peter, and this is my brother,
Andrew.

31

JAMES
I'm James, and my brother there is John.

JESUS
How has the fishing been?

PETER
Not bad--but not good. We're catching up on
some repairs today.

JESUS
But you'll go fishing again tomorrow?

JOHN
Yes.

JESUS
Follow me--and I'll make you fishers of men.

ANDREW
Do you mean right now?

JESUS
Yes, right now.

ANDREW
Well, I don't know about that.

PETER
Didn't you hear what he was preaching? I think
I might go.

Two of the men from the crowd come in a little closer
and begin talking to Jesus.

FIRST MAN
Teacher, I'll follow you, but let me go back
home first and say farewell to my family.

JESUS
No one who puts his hand to the plough and
looks back is fit for the kingdom of God.

SECOND MAN
I will follow you, but I've got to go and bury
my father first.

JESUS
Leave the dead to bury their own dead and you
come proclaim the kingdom of God.

SECOND MAN
Well, if you can't take time to bury your own
father, what can you take time for?

JESUS
For following me.

SECOND MAN
That undermines the law and violates true
piety.

JESUS
You'll have to decide whether that's true.

PETER
If we do come, we'll have to leave our work.
What'll we do for money?

JESUS
We'll figure that out as we go along.

ANDREW
Where did you say we were going?

JESUS
The foxes have holes, and the birds of the air
have nests, but I have nowhere to lay my head.
If you come along, it'll be to nowhere to lay
your head.

ANDREW
I'm glad you cleared that up.

JAMES
I don't know why, but I think I'm going.

PETER
Let's all go.

ANDREW
I'm coming.

JOHN
Teacher, my father is fifty feet away working
on his nets (pointing). Do you think I could
go over and tell him good-by?

JESUS
Go ahead--but don't waste any time.

33

James and John move to tell their father good-by. While they step over there, Peter yells to him.

                    PETER
Hey, Zebedee, we're going to be fishers of men.

The four walk off down the road with Jesus into Capernaum.

                      2.

    A few days later Jesus' small house in Capernaum is packed with people who have come to hear him preach. Four men have brought their paralyzed friend, and because of the crowd around the door they have taken their friend up the outside stairway, dug a hole through the roof, let the pallet down into the midst of the room near where Jesus is standing, and then they have also come through the hole into Jesus' presence. With a benignly quizzical expression Jesus glances at the hole in his roof and then looks at the four men.

                    JESUS
That was quite an act of faith.

                ONE OF THE FOUR
How so? We just heard that someone kind of like John the Baptist was preachimg here but saying different things. We thought you might be able to heal our friend. No one can help him.

                    JESUS
But you think I can?

                ONE OF THE FOUR
We don't know. We just hope so. Can you?

                    JESUS
             (to the paralytic)
My brother, your sins are forgiven.

                ANOTHER OF THE FOUR
He doesn't want to be forgiven. He just wants to walk.

                    JESUS
             (to the paralytic)
Do you want to be forgiven?

                      34

THE PARALYTIC

Well, teacher, I've been so concerned about being paralyzed I hadn't given a lot of thought to being guilty.

JESUS

Do you suppose there's a connection?

THE PARALYTIC

There may be. If you're sure I'm forgiven, I'll consider being a sinner.

JESUS

You **are** forgiven, but God wants your **whole** body to be well--so rise, pick up your pallet and go home.

The paralytic, looking amazed and joyful, gets up and makes his way through the crowd to the door, carrying his pallet. As he is leaving Asa, the scribe, begins speaking heatedly to those around him.

ASA

Did you hear him? Did you hear what this Jesus said? "Your sins are forgiven." It's an outrage, only God can forgive sins!

MAN IN THE CROWD

It's a new teaching. He speaks with authority.

ASA

Why does this man say such things? He blas-phemes against God.

MAN IN THE CROWD

It's amazing! I never saw anything like this. Teacher, won't you stay in Capernaum?

JESUS

No, but I'll be back. Now I must go to the other towns and preach in them, too. That's why I came out. There's not much time to get through the cities of Israel.

3.

Passing along the seashore with his disciples,

Jesus has called Levi, the tax collector, to join the band, and the latter has abandoned his lucrative, if dishonest job, to do so. Now Jesus and his other disciples are gathered at Levi's house where the host is entertaining them, as well as a group of his old friends--tax collectors and sinners--at a dinner. It is a noisy and rowdy group.

                    LEVI
Eat heartily, gentlemen, the last course is about to be served.

                    ANDREW
This is the best meal I've had since we took to the road with the teacher.

                    JAMES
The food's good, but the crowd's another question.

                    JOHN
Who are these people anyway?

                    ANDREW
Friends of the host--obviously. Friends of Levi, our newest brother.

                    JOHN
We've never been all that careful about piety around our house--but this bunch is ridiculous.

                    JAMES
I never thought Jesus would actually call a tax collector to follow with us.

                    PETER
Why not?

                    JOHN
Because they're thieves--and traitors--that's why not.

                    PETER
It doesn't seem to bother the teacher. He's really talking to them, especially to that fellow, Bartholomew.

                    JOHN
The next thing you know Bartholomew will be one
of us.

Two servants begin clearing away dishes and bringing
in the last course. As this occurs Asa, the scribe,
slips in with three companions.

                    ASA
          (to the disciples)
Why does your teacher eat with tax collectors
and sinners?

                    JESUS
          (overhearing, walks down
           to where Asa is)
Because I'm hungry.

                    ASA
I didn't mean why do you eat--Sir (with acid
sarcasm). I meant why with them.

                    JESUS
Because it's the sick who need a physician--not
the well.

                    ASA
They don't look sick to me.   Their appetites
are healthy enough.

                    JESUS
But what about their hearts?   Don't their
hearts--our hearts--need something? Something
given by what we share here--the food, good
feelings, even the revelry.

                    ASA
But you could teach the righteous and eat with
them, those who are zealous for the law. After
all they deserve a little comfort and con-
solation. And they can always be led to even
greater obedience.

                    JESUS
The righteous don't seem to be hearing my word--
the   word   the   kingdom   brings   them.

                    ASA
In that case they wouldn't really be righteous.

                              JESUS
Precisely!

                              ASA
If the righteous aren't righteous, who is? If
obedience doesn't tell you who is righteous,
what good is the law?

                             JESUS
That's what we're trying to find out.

Jesus turns around and goes back to his dinner companions, and as Asa and his friends leave, the scribe
speaks to them.

                              ASA
We may have to deal with him.

                            PETER
                     (to the disciples)
I'm glad we came though I don't know where it's
going. It seems shaky as hell to me.

                            JAMES
Maybe we should go back to fishing--for fish.

                            PETER
But how can we not follow him? I've got to find
out what's going on with him. Sometimes he
seems like the most intense person I've ever
met. And at other times I feel like he's
watching a play in the theatre--or acting in
one.

                          ANDREW
Well, let's stick with it a while longer.

                           JOHN
I'm going to spend some time with my wife next
week. I can tell you that right now.

                          PETER
It does seem important. (musing) We're trying
to find out what good the law is. If I don't
know that, I don't know exactly where I am.
Maybe I'm one of the sick--one of the sick made
well.

4.

Some weeks later Jesus and his disciples (he has now added Bartholomew and two others to the company) are walking down the road on a sabbath day. Because the disciples are hungry, they stop and walk a few feet into a grain field to pluck some ears of grain. While they are in the midst of picking and eating, Asa, the scribe, and ten or twelve companions appear on the scene.

                         ASA
                    (to Jesus)
Look here, why are your followers breaking the law?

                        JESUS
The law says an Israelite can satisfy his hunger in a neighbor's field.

                         ASA
But it's the sabbath, man. They're breaking the sabbath, they're reaping grain. The sabbath is one of the great gifts God has given us. You can't be a true Israelite and not keep the sabbath.

                        JESUS
Haven't you ever read that David the king and his men went into the house of God and ate the bread that was lawful only for priests to eat-- just because they were hungry.

                         ASA
They were on the point of death.

                        JESUS
You don't know that. Perhaps they were just hungry. But however that may be, the sabbath was made for human beings, not human beings for the sabbath.

                         ASA
But what right do you have to say that? Who do you think you are to destroy the law and not even give us a sign from heaven to prove your authority?

                    JESUS
It's a sinful and adulterous generation that
wants a sign--and you're not going to get it--
unless the sign of Jonah.

                    ANDREW
Well, that was a miraculous sign. Jonah lived
three days and nights in the belly of a big
fish--and then the fish puked him up on dry
land...I mean--the Lord delivered him.

                    JESUS
That was not the sign of Jonah. Jonah's sign
was his preaching to Nineveh, and my sign to
you is the preaching of the reign of God.

As this conversation has been developing a number of
passers-by on the road have stopped to listen.

                    ASA
Kingdom of God or no kingdom of God you're
destroying the law.

                    JESUS
No, I'm fulfilling it. I'm concerned about
what God intended for us in the law. It means
more than it says.

                    JAMES
What's that?

                    JESUS
You've heard it said in the law: You shall not
kill and whoever kills will be liable to
judgment. But I tell you: Everyone who is
angry with his brother, everyone who insults
his brother, everyone who calls him a fool,
will be liable to the hell of fire. You've
heard it said: You shall not commit adultery.
But I tell you. Everyone who looks at a woman
lustfully has already committed adultery with
her in his heart. You've heard it in the law:
You shall not swear falsely but shall perform
to the Lord what you have sworn. But I say to
you: Do not swear at all. If every yes means
yes and every no means no, why should there be
any more?

                            40

                    PETER
                (interrupting)
But I thought the law calls on us to take oaths
and keep them. The fulfilling of the law seems
to cancel it out.

                    JESUS
That's a possibility....And you've heard it
said: You shall love your neighbor and hate
your enemy.   But I tell you: love your enemy,
pray for the person who persecutes you so you
may be children of your Father in heaven--who
makes his sun shine and his rain fall on both
the just and the unjust.

                    ANDREW
Well, that's asking a lot.

                    JAMES
And I really don't see why thinking about it,
or wanting to do it in your heart, is the same
thing as doing it.   After all, I'd rather old
Andrew here not hate me, but if I have to
choose between him hating me and killing me,
I'll take hating.   It wouldn't hurt me near as
much.

                    JESUS
But maybe it would hurt him as much--to do it
to you in his heart as to do it to you with his
hand.   You know the rabbis tell us we have a
heart from above--we get it from our fathers.
When that heart makes our own heart feel the
pain of guilt, it doesn't distinguish between
what we've done and what we've thought and
felt.

The disciples and others in the crowd all look at each
other with puzzled faces.

                    JAMES
                (to the other disciples)
I've never heard the rabbis say anything like
that.   The teacher's said some odd things
before, but that doesn't make any sense at all.
(to Jesus) Teacher, do you need to slow down
and take a rest, or were you trying to tell us
something?

                         JESUS
I am telling you something. A good tree can
only produce good fruit and a bad tree, bad
fruit. Only if your hearts are good can your
acts be good.

                         PETER
He's trying to tell us God wants us totally--
our hearts and our deeds, and our deeds match
our hearts.

                         JESUS
Exactly. You can't get figs from thorns or
grapes from a bramble bush.

                         ANDREW
God is demanding everything from us. Is there
no place to escape to? Is there any place
where he's not there asking everything of us?

                         JESUS
Not really. Some have even made themselves
eunuchs for the sake of the kingdom.

                         JOHN
Eunuchs! Eunuchs! Good god, we've given up our
jobs and left home. We've been walking the hell
all over Galilee--and now he wants us to cut
off our peters for the kingdom.

                         JAMES
It seems like Peter's becoming our leader. Why
don't we let him represent us? Let's just cut
off Peter's peter.

A playfully villainous grin breaks out on John's face.

                         JOHN
Hey, man, he's our leader, let's all cut off
Peter's peter.

The disciples all begin to laugh uproariously and,
looking at Peter, they chant in unison:

    Hey, man, he's our leader, let's all cut off
    Peter's--

Suddenly they stop without completing the sentence as
if all struck at the same instant with wonderment

                          42

about what Jesus must be thinking. Slowly and apprehensively they turn their gaze toward Jesus--to be met
by his questioning, ironical, forbearing smile.

                         JESUS
    I'm glad you haven't lost your capacity for
    humor, brothers. But be serious while you
    laugh. I'm not giving you new laws, you know,
    so don't take me too literally. Parables are a
    lot more fun than laws, and a lot more dif-
    ficult to understand--and a lot more demanding.
    So give the light a chance. Let the lamp shine
    on the lampstand and not under the bed.

                          5.

    Jesus and his now twelve disciples have arrived
in the city of Tiberias. They walk into a busy square
and stop, looking around. A dirty, disheveled figure
with a wild look in his eye is standing nearby, gazing
into the distance.

                         JAMES
                    (to Jesus)
    There're an awful lot of gentiles in Tiberias.
    Are you going to cast your pearls before them?

                         JESUS
    Very probably. There are plenty of gentile
    sinners, but maybe they'll listen better than
    Israelites.

                         JAMES
                    (to Jesus, pointing to
                     the dirty man)
    That poor bastard's got a demon.

                        ANDREW
    How do you know?

                         JAMES
    Look at him, fool, he--

                        ANDREW
                    (interrupting)
    Don't call me a fool!

                         JAMES
    Well, look at him, dummy. He's filthy, he's

                          43

foaming at the mouth--and other places. He's
waving his arms and talking to someone who's
not there.

Jesus walks over to the demoniac who is speaking gib-
berish into the air. More people have gathered.

                    JESUS
              (to the demoniac)
Who are you?

                    DEMONIAC
What's it to you? Why are you here before the
time?

                    JESUS
I'm here to put you out, so come out of this
man, you unclean demon!

The man falls on the ground, convulsed. Asa and
twelve or fifteen companions have arrived and wit-
nessed this scene. They, Jesus, and the disciples
watch the demoniac as his body shakes and then becomes
still. After a moment he stands up with an expression
of peaceful calm on his face.

                    JESUS
Well, Asa, I didn't think you'd pursue me into
Tiberias.   Aren't you afraid you'll get
contaminated?

                    ASA
One may have to risk something to protect the
law.

                    JESUS
And you're risking your purity.

                    ASA
Yes. And I think you have Satan, you have
Beelzebul. It's by the prince of the demons
that you cast out demons.

                    JESUS
No, it's not by Satan. He's no fool. He
wouldn't be at war with himself. It's by the
Spirit that I cast out demons because the reign
of God has come.

ASA

It's not the kingdom of God. You commit
blasphemy, break the sabbath, eat with sinners.
You haven't come near the kingdom.

JESUS

You know how to interpret the sky, Asa. You
know a cloud in the west means rain. You know
a south wind means heat. Why don't you know
how to interpret the present time? You've concealed the truth from yourself so long you
can't see what's going on. Why don't you know
what time it is?

ASA

I do know. It's always time to obey God. The
gall of you to suggest you bring the kingdom!
You do have a demon.

JESUS

Asa, will you ever find forgiveness? Will you
ever discern the difference between what the
Spirit is doing and what the demons are doing?
You talk about blasphemy and breaking the law
and eating with sinners. Will you ever see
beneath the surface and discover what's going
on?

While Jesus is saying this Mary, his mother, and his
four brothers edge up to the crowd around Jesus,
within earshot but unseen by Jesus.

JOHN

I know what's going on, and I know what time it
is. It's time to go home.

James, Jesus' brother, has been making his way up
closer to where Jesus is standing. Others have joined
the crowd.

JESUS

He who loves home or parents, son or daughter,
more than me is not worthy of me. I didn't
come to bring peace but a sword. I'll set a
man against his father and a woman against her
mother.

JAMES, JESUS' BROTHER

Jesus!

45

                    JESUS
James, I'm glad to see you--and surprised.

                    JAMES
Yes, I'm sure. What could you care less about
than your family? This message of yours is even
worse than I might have expected.

                    JESUS
The new time is bursting forth upon us, James.
If anyone comes to me and doesn't hate his own
father and mother and wife and children and
brothers and sisters, yes, and even his own
life, he can't be my disciple.

                    JAMES
That's repugnant, Jesus.   You're undermining
the family and wrecking the community.   What
kind of person would want to be your disciple
when you're out of your mind?

                    JESUS
Well, I'll have to leave the latter point up to
you. But I'm not impairing the commumity. All
these around me are my mother and brothers and
sisters, those who extend God's love, and are
open to his future.

                    JAMES
But what about the community knit together by
God's law, what about the natural family and
birth and tradition?

                    JESUS
The coming of the kingdom creates new rela-
tionships, James.

                    JAMES
The inauguration of chaos and disorder is not
the kingdom of God.

                    PETER
But the healing of the sick and the driving out
of demons is.

                    JAMES
The kingdom can't be so many things at once.

                         JESUS
Perhaps it can.

                        DEMONIAC
                  (who has been listening
                     intently)
Am I your brother, sir?

                         JESUS
You are indeed. Come follow with us. There is
no one who has left home and family for my sake
and the gospel's who will not receive houses
and brothers and sisters a hundredfold in this
time--with persecution--and in the age to come
eternal life.

The crowd in the square around Jesus has been joined
by a woman--dirty and dressed in tatters, her hair is
matted and unkempt. As she looks at Jesus with a
desolate yet wistful expression, some of the disciples
watch her. They are also in the crowd but some little
distance away.

                         JAMES
                  (motioning toward the woman
                     with his head)
Look at that flea bag. God, what a mess.

                        ANDREW
She's sure eyeing the lord.

                         JAMES
Who's the lord?

                        ANDREW
Jesus...the teacher. Who else?

                         JAMES
Why'd you call him the lord?

                        ANDREW
I don't know.

                         JAMES
Then why did you say it?

                         PETER
Maybe we'll find out--if our ears are open.

                          47

JOHN

Well, maybe so, but look at that woman. What
do you suppose is wrong with her?

JAMES

I don't know, but I bet she stinks.

PETER

Maybe she has a bleeding problem and she's
unclean.

ANDREW

Do you think she'll try to touch the teacher?

JAMES

I'd hate to have the nasty thing touch me.

PETER

I don't believe Jesus would mind.

JOHN

Of course not. If she did touch him, the power
would just flow right out of him--and heal her
on the spot.

Jesus begins to walk away with people pressing closely
around him, and as he passes the woman, she reaches
out apprehensively and touches him. He stops and
looks around.

JESUS

Who touched me?

BARTHOLOMEW

What do you mean, who touched you? There're
people bumping you all over the place.

JESUS

I'm not talking about bumping. I'm talking
about touching. Who?

WOMAN
(hesitatingly)
I touched you, sir.

JESUS

Why?

WOMAN

Because I've had a hemorrhage for twelve years,

and I've spent all my money on doctors, and I'm
worse than I was at the beginning. I heard
about you and I thought that if I even touched
your cloak I'd be healed.... And I believe I
have been.

                    JESUS
Sister, your faith has made you well, and the
kingdom of God has come. Go your way in peace.

Peter, Andrew and the others have walked up to where
Jesus and the woman are.

                    ANDREW
Teacher, I still don't think we've got the
kingdom of God.

                    JAMES
Neither do I. We don't really understand it.

                    JESUS
Maybe you haven't got the kingdom because the
kingdom hasn't got you. But I'll explain it to
you in simple terms. The land of a rich man
produced plentifully, and he thought to himself, "What shall I do, for I have nowhere to
store my crops?" Then he said, "I'll do this.
I'll pull down my barns and build bigger ones,
and there I'll store all my grain and goods.
And I'll say to myself, 'Self, you've got
plenty of stuff to last a hundred years. Take
it easy, and, eat, drink and be merry.'" But
God said to him, "Fool, this night your soul is
required of you."

                    JAMES
We aren't rich, so it doesn't have anything to
do with us.

                    PETER
But we all have to die.

                    JOHN
Are we supposed to think about that every day?

                    JESUS
That might not be as depressing as you think.

ANDREW

Why not?

JESUS

It will free you.

JOHN

From what?

JESUS

From trivia--and from the impossible.

JAMES

So what do we do while we're thinking about our
death and getting freed?

PETER

We do everything. We do everything important
because that's what you'd do the day before you
died.

JAMES

Then we'd get a good reward.

JESUS

If you had a servant plowing or keeping sheep
and he came in from the field at night, would
you invite him to sit right down at the table
and eat?   No, you'd say to him, "Prepare my
supper and put on your apron and serve me.
Then after I've eaten and drunk, you can do the
same." Would you then thank your servant for
all that obedience?   So you, too, when you've
done everything important, everything commanded
you, you can only say "We're unworthy servants;
nobody's going to thank us; we've only done our
duty."

JAMES

Then to hell with the whole thing.

JESUS

Not necessarily. Two men went up to the temple
to pray, one a pharisee and the other a tax
collector. The pharisee stood by himself and
said, "God, I thank you that I am not like
other men, extortioners, unjust, adulterers, or
even like this tax collector. I fast twice a

week and give tithes on all I get." But the
tax collector, standing far off, would not even
lift up his eyes to heaven, but beat his breast
saying, "God be merciful to me a sinner." Which
one of the two men had God accepted?

Jesus' family has made its way into the circle close
to Jesus.

JAMES, JESUS' BROTHER
That's not too hard to guess. With you, Jesus,
of course it's the sinner.

PETER
We all want the sinner's role, that is, we all
want mercy--when we don't have any righteous-
ness to stand on.

JAMES
(to Peter)
It's enough that I have to hear this affront to
piety from Jesus! Do I have to hear it from
you, too?

PETER
You don't **have** to hear it from anybody. You
can leave.

JESUS
Ah, let him stay. I still have parables to
tell. There was a rich man who had a steward
and charges were brought to him that this man
was wasting his goods. And he called him in
and said to him, "What's this that I hear about
you? Turn in your records; you're about to be
fired." So the steward said to himself, "What
shall I do in the face of this nasty turn of
events? I'm not strong enough to dig, and I'm
ashamed to beg. I've decided what to do so
that I'll have some place to turn when I'm out
in the cold." Then summoning his master's deb-
tors one by one he said to the first, "How much
do you owe my master?" He said, "A hundred
measures of oil." And the steward said, "Take
your note and sit down quickly and write
fifty." Then he said to another, "And how much
do you owe?" He replied, "A hundred measures
of wheat." The steward said to him, "Take your

note and write eighty." And so it went until
the master discovered what was going on;
whereupon he commended the dishonest steward
for his prudence.

                    ANDREW
Why would the master praise the steward? He
just got taken by him.

                    JESUS
Sometimes people surpass themselves when you
least expect it.

          JAMES, JESUS' BROTHER
But the steward was a cheat.

                    JESUS
That's not all, but let's concede he was a
cheat. Can't you enjoy identifying with a
cheat, James--for a moment? Give your seamy
side a fling.

                    JAMES
I'm more serious about my duty than that.

                    JESUS
Must the kingdom come with dead seriousness?

                    JOHN
The steward **was** a thief.

                    PETER
But he knew what time it was.

                    JOHN
What time was it?

                    JESUS
That's what I've been telling you.

                    JOHN
I didn't hear you. I just heard some strange
stories. Why **do** you tell these parables
anyway, Teacher?

                    JESUS
In order that those on the outside may indeed
see but not perceive and may indeed hear but

not understand, lest they turn around and find
forgiveness.

                    PETER
Who's on the outside?

                    JESUS
Those who don't understand.

              JAMES, THE DISCIPLE
              (who has been whispering to
              Andrew during the last
              exchange)
Why did you say you tell these parables?

                    JESUS
To make a lamp shine in the darkness and bring
the hidden things to light.

                    PETER
I thought you said it was to hide the light.

                    JESUS
I did. I tell them to hide the light unless
you see it.

                    JAMES
You've succeeded again, Teacher. We've really
got it now.

                    JESUS
Then it's been a good day.

                    6.

     Jesus, some weeks later, has returned to Nazareth
with his disciples, followed by Asa, the scribe, and
about twenty of his supporters. His tracking of Jesus
has now become a regular pattern. Outside the synagogue Jesus is surrounded by his disciples, Asa and
his friends, and a rather large group of citizens of
Nazareth.

                    JAMES
The sabbath's almost over, Teacher, and we
haven't broken any laws. We'd better get busy.

                    JESUS
The sabbath's for keeping, James, not breaking--

                    53

unless you understand why.

                         JOHN
Oh, we understand all right. Are you going to
talk to this crowd? They seem curious, they
want to hear you. But you know the old saying
--a prophet is not without honor except in his
own country.

                         JESUS
I know the saying. Where do you think I've
been? But I have some things to say to
Nazareth--even if I wasn't asked to preach in
the synagogue.

                       TOWNSMAN
Are you going to shock us, Jesus--now that
you've come back to Nazareth? We hear you've
been offending people all around Galilee.

                         JESUS
If the way the kingdom comes offends you,
you'll be offended. But really I bring you
good news. (now more loudly so that all can
hear) Don't be anxious about your life, what
you'll eat or what you'll drink, or about your
body--what you'll put on it. Isn't life more
than food and the body more than clothes? Look
at the birds of the air--they neither sow nor
reap nor gather into barns, but your heavenly
father feeds them. Aren't you more valuable
than they are? Can being anxious add a day to
your life?   And why all the concern about
clothes? Consider the lilies of the field.
They neither toil nor spin, but Solomon in all
his glory was not arrayed like one of these.
Don't be anxious about what you're going to eat
or drink or put on your back. Your heavenly
father knows you need these things, so seek
his kingdom first.

                       TOWNSMAN
Then we should just quit work!

                         JESUS
That's not quite it.

SECOND TOWNSMAN
Then what is it?

JESUS
If you consider your neighbor's need, you'll
understand your own risk.

TOWNSMAN
But what's the point of gambling? Our wives and
children need food and clothes. It's hard
enough to stay alive without taking chances.
You have to think about tomorrow.

JESUS
No, tomorrow is what you have not to think
about.

SECOND TOWNSMAN
Why, for god's sake?

JESUS
Because thinking about it conceals the reality
of today.

SECOND TOWNSMAN
Well, it hasn't concealed the reality of this
day. I can certainly see what's going on. You
come back here with this offensive message--

JESUS
(interrupting)
God himself does startling things.

FIRST TOWNSMAN
We have a right not to be startled.

JESUS
Oh.

SECOND TOWNSMAN
You come back here as if we didn't know who you
are--the carpenter, the son of Mary. We've
seen you grow up here--and go off--and come
back--and go off again--and come back again.
Where did you get all this? You act like
you've been given some special message that's
supposed to turn our world upside down.

55

ASA

He wants us to risk everything for God, but he
himself won't show God the least reverence.
Not even will he fast. Why don't you fast,
Jesus? The disciples of John fast and so do
the Pharisees. But not you, Jesus, and not
your disciples. Why don't you fast?

JESUS

Can the wedding guests fast when the bridegroom
is with them? If you'd let tomorrow take care
of itself, you'd know what today is.

A messenger has been coming down the street and just
as Jesus finishes speaking he begins to call out to
the crowd around Jesus.

MESSENGER

The sun is down, and the sabbath's over. Come
to the wedding feast. You're all invited, no
one's excluded. Today is a day of celebration.
My master's son is taking a bride. Come to the
marriage feast.

The whole crowd, including Jesus and his disciples,
follows the messenger down the street, talking
noisily.

7.

A large crowd is moving around in a spacious
courtyard--eating, drinking, and talking. The air is
very festive.

ANDREW

This is the best food I've had in a long time.

PETER

The best since Levi's party the day he joined
the band.

JAMES

And the wine's not bad either.

ANDREW

How did we--and all these others--happen to get
invited to this party anyway? That messenger
just brought in everyone off the streets.

56

                         JESUS
I'm told that all the original guests--the
people of position in Nazareth--were all too
busy to come. The host wasn't going to be
thwarted, so he decided to invite whoever could
be found--and here we are--and let us enjoy it.

                        ANDREW
I hear the wine's about to run out already. A
lot more people came than he expected.

                         JESUS
The wine merchant around the corner is an old
friend of mine, makes the best wine in
Nazareth. James, take three or four of the
others and go get a couple of big jars and
bring them back. Tell him I'll settle with him
later.

James and four other disciples leave to get the wine.

                        ANDREW
Man, the lord's going to look after us.

                         JOHN
What's this about the lord again?

                        ANDREW
It's time you knew.

Another guest who has been observing this conversation
walks up to Jesus.

                         GUEST
Did you send out for more wine?

                         JESUS
Yes.

                         GUEST
Why?

                         JESUS
For what possible reason? What's a feast
without wine?

A loud knocking is heard on the closed door of the
courtyard, and everyone's attention turns toward the
door as the host walks toward it.

                    JOHN
              (to his friends around him)
      Who could that be?

The host opens the door and a female voice can be
heard from outside.

                    VOICE
      Sir, may we come in? We were invited by your
      messenger, but we had to stop in the market on
      the way. We needed oil for our lamps. But we
      like parties. May we come in?

                    HOST
      It's too late now, you should have come when
      you could. The door's been shut, so you can't
      come in. I tell you I never knew you.

The door is shut as everyone watches.

                    JOHN
              (to Jesus)
      Why'd he do that?

                    JESUS
      The door had been shut, and the feast was
      underway. They'd had their chance to get in.

                    PETER
      But it's a feast. Everybody's having a good
      time. He invited everybody anyway, so why turn
      some people away? It didn't hurt if they were
      a little late. This is a party. It doesn't
      fit.

                    JESUS
      Perhaps it does. You never know whether your
      present chance is your last chance--for a
      celebration....Where are James and the others?
      They should be getting back.

A knock is heard at the door, and everyone looks
toward it. A servant of the host then admits James
and his companions bringing in two large jars of wine.

                        58

                    SERVANT
               (to James)
What's this for?

                     JAMES
You were running out of wine. Didn't you know
it?

                    SERVANT
No, I've been busy.

                     JAMES
Well, you were, so here's some more. The
teacher had it sent for.

                    SERVANT
Why should he?

                     JAMES
He seems to like a party, especially a wedding
feast. He'll surprise you.

Jesus walks over to where they are.

                     JESUS
So you're back. How is it?

                     JAMES
We haven't tried it yet.

                     JESUS
Then try it. (calls to the crowd) Come, my
friends. There's more wine.

A number of people rush over with their cups and have
them filled.

                     GUEST
               (after drinking a few swallows)
This is good, better than what we had at first.

                 SECOND GUEST
               (tries his)
It's great. And think, we might not have come.

                  FIRST GUEST
We didn't exactly come. We were just kind of

swept in. We all were.

                    SECOND GUEST
However..... we're here.

The host has walked over to this little group.

                    FIRST GUEST
              (to host)
Sir, you saved the best wine for last. Why'd
you do that?

                    THIRD GUEST
              (to first guest)
How would you know which is best--as much as
you've drunk?

                    FIRST GUEST
I know.

                    HOST
I didn't know there was a new supply.

                    JESUS
I had it brought in. You were very busy.

                    HOST
Whose feast is it? Are you the host?

                    JESUS
No, of course not. I'm just a helper. It was
something I could do.

                    HOST
              (recognizing Jesus)
Why, you're our wandering prophet. You're much
more than a helper. Of course....You're our
prophet returned to his home town (with growing
sarcasm).

                    JESUS
That sounds like an accurate description.

                    HOST
I hear you have quite a demanding message.
We're to love our enemies--including Samari-
tans. No anger, nothing but truth, purity of

heart. Is that the kind of message that goes along with supplying the wine?

                    JESUS
A marriage feast needs wine.

                    HOST
I'm the host, I can provide the wine. You're only a guest, and just barely one at that. It was luck.

                    JESUS
I recognize the good fortune. It seemed fitting to be grateful.

                    HOST
It's fitting for a glutton and a drunk (calling to his servants). Take him by his hands and feet and throw him out!

The servants manhandle Jesus and put him out the door. The disciples follow.

                    8.

     Jesus has taken his disciples to the north Galilean town of Gischala, near the Phoenician border. They have just finished a meal in a small outdoor restaurant and Jesus is still sitting at the table with two or three disciples. The others are milling around in the street with the crowd, and several of them begin talking, at some distance from Jesus.

                    JAMES
Why'd the teacher bring us all the way up here? The next thing you know he'll be going across the border and preaching to the gentiles (assuming a dramatic pose): Ah, Tyre and Sidon, Ah, people of Phoenicia, the kingdom of God has come for you--and his blessings are poured out upon you.

                    JOHN
We're here because we got our asses thrown out of the best party in Nazareth.

                    PETER
He brought us up here because he wanted to get

away from the pressures and the constant attacks and plan our future.

                    JOHN
Well, he didn't bring us far enough because here come Asa and his henchmen.

Asa and some thirty people appear, including scribes from Jerusalem. They walk over to Jesus, and Asa begins the conversation. Peter has also walked over to where Jesus and Asa are.

                    ASA
You're a little far from the normal territory, aren't you?

                    JESUS
Well, it's not as far from home for me as it is for you. Who are your new friends?

                    ASA
They're from Jerusalem--that should interest you. So, you've been eating again.

                    JESUS
I eat from time to time.

                    ASA
I thought maybe you miracle workers didn't have to.

                    JESUS
Oh, yes, we have to. In fact I try to eat regularly.

                    ASA
And of course, you don't bother to wash your hands, or have your disciples wash theirs.

                    JESUS
No, I don't. Why should I?

                    ASA
Why should you? You know very well why you should. You know the law as well as I do. Don't act dumb.

                    JESUS
Where does Scripture say I must wash my hands before I eat?

ASA

It's in the tradition of the elders. And as
you well know, that also came from Moses.

JESUS

Where it came from is not the issue. What it
means is.

ASA

Eating with unwashed hands makes you unclean.

JESUS

No, it doesn't. (calling to the crowd) Hear
me, all of you, and understand. There is
nothing that goes into a person from outside
that can defile him or make him unclean before
God.

PETER

Then the kingdom of God is freedom. We don't
have to obey the ritual laws. We're freed from
the fear of being unclean because we touch
something or eat something.

BYSTANDER

Then we can live like gentiles.

JESUS

I hope so. I've found some gentiles responsive
to my preaching.

BYSTANDER

I don't know about that. I mean if we can't be
defiled, let's live like gentiles--fornicate,
lie, steal--fornicate.

SECOND BYSTANDER

Yes, that's the way they are--especially the
Phoenicians--and more especially the women.

JESUS

They're not all like that and neither are you
to be. You're not defiled by what goes in your
mouth, but you are by what comes out of your
heart, by cultivating the evil intentions of
your own hearts. You're made unclean by the
murder and theft and adultery and greed and
deceit and pride that come from within and
infect the world.

There's a slight commotion on the edge of the crowd as a woman begins talking to Jesus' disciples.

                    WOMAN
     I'd like to go up and talk to your teacher.

                    ANDREW
     Who are you?

                    WOMAN
     I'm a Phoenician. I live between here and
     Tyre. I've heard about the compassion of this
     man Jesus.

                    ANDREW
     What do you want?

                    WOMAN
     I need to ask something of him.

                    ANDREW
     Can't you speak Aramaic?

                    WOMAN
     Not really. I only speak Greek.

                    ANDREW
     He can speak Greek. Come along.

Andrew leads her up to where Jesus is.

                    ANDREW
     Teacher, this Phoenician woman wants to ask you
     something.

                    JESUS
     We were just speaking of Phoenician women.
     What do you want?

                    WOMAN
     My daughter is possessed by an unclean spirit.
     Will you cast the demon out?

                    JESUS
     Will I?   I don't know.   I've seen respon-
     siveness in gentiles. But you're the first
     actually to ask me for healing. Should I?
     Israel still needs to be fed. Is it right to

take the bread from the children and throw it
to the dogs?

> WOMAN
> (with a certain irony)
> But, Sir, even the dogs under the table eat the
> children's crumbs...(pauses, then with vehe-
> mence) But why **should** they? Why should they
> eat the crumbs under the table? Why should we?
> You just said yourself it's the inside that
> counts, not the outside.

Jesus looks intently at her face, but she averts her
eyes.

> WOMAN (cont.)
> Suppose we are righteous within.

Now she looks back directly into Jesus' eyes.

> WOMAN (cont.)
> Suppose my heart has known love....Suppose my
> eyes have rejoiced in the sun's gold--left in
> the sky above a Syrian hillside.

> ANDREW
> What does that have to do with her daughter?

> JESUS
> My sister, you may go your way. The demon has
> left your daughter.... Let me, indeed, walk a
> way with you.

They walk away from the crowd, not looking at each
other but clearly together. Conversation begins to
buzz around Asa, and all heads turn in his direction. Just beyond the edge of the crowd Jesus and the
woman stop and look into each other's faces. They
touch hands.

> JESUS
> Chara, you **are** my love.

> WOMAN
> Jesus, you **are** my life.

The woman walks away and Jesus walks back toward Asa.

ASA
(loudly to his cohorts)
Look at him. I wasn't exaggerating. Not only
does he break the law in every conceivable way.
He also consorts with Phoenician women. Of
course, the worst offense is that he violates
the law of Israel's God, but let it not be lost
on you, my friends from Jerusalem, his disre-
gard for the law will cause disorder among the
people, and our leaders will be in trouble with
Rome if they can't keep the peace.

He sees that Jesus is now close by.

ASA (cont.)
We are going to deal with you.

JESUS
And ultimately, in one way or another I will
deal with you, and with all of Israel.

9.

Jesus has led the disciples still farther north
to the region of Caesarea Philippi, outside of
Galilee. They stop by the roadside for a rest.

JOHN
What happened to the mission to Israel anyway?
We've left Galilee behind on our trek north.

JESUS
Don't think I've forgotten my people. We'll
turn south soon enough. But, apart from Asa
and his friends, how do you think Israel is
responding to my mission? Who do they say I
am?

ANDREW
They think you're John the Baptist raised from
the dead.

JAMES
Some of them think you're Elijah or one of the
other prophets returned.

JESUS
But who do you think I am?

                    PETER
              (confidently)
We know--you're the Messiah, the Son of God.

                    JESUS
No....no, I'm not. And you mustn't say it.

                    PETER
              (with shocked disbelief)
But why aren't you the Messiah?

                    JESUS
Because being the Messiah would be like giving
the scribes a miraculous sign when they ask for
one in unbelief. The Messiah's role is defin-
ed. He is who he is and everyone knows who he
is, so he already has authority.

                    JAMES
But you have authority. How can you not be the
Messiah? You've called us from our jobs to
follow you. You said we had to decide right
now. You've claimed authority to change the
law and made impossible demands upon us. Who
are you then if you're not the Messiah? What
are you?

                    JESUS
What doesn't come into the picture--because I'm
still finding out who I am myself.

                    ANDREW
Then how can we believe in you--if you're not
the Messiah?

                    JESUS
You'll just have to take a chance that my
preaching and the way of life I'm leading you
into is right.

                    PETER
But surely you know who are you.

                    JESUS
Yes, in a way I know who. I've studied the
Scriptures, I've read about the prophets and
holy men. I can see what happened to John the
Baptist, I'm not oblivious to what has happened

to myself. I'm going to suffer for this mission. In fact, I'm going to die for it--but I believe that somehow God will vindicate me.

PETER

No! You are not to die. You've given us what we most deeply need. You've brought us forgiveness for our sins. You've given healing to hurt bodies and peace to souls tormented by the demons. You've freed us from the law and pointed us down a new way. All of that will be lost if you die. You cannot die.

JESUS

Get behind me, Satan.

PETER

Satan? You're calling me Satan?

JESUS

Peter, you've often understood me better than anyone. But now you're trying to turn me from the way I've been given--the way into which I've called all of you. Is that the problem? Don't you want to walk this way?

JOHN

I don't think we really knew exactly where it was you were going.

JESUS

I thought you did, but maybe I wasn't paying attention. I thought it was becoming as clear to you as it was to me. Whoever tries to save his life will lose it, but whoever loses his life for the sake of the kingdom of God will find it. There's not much time, God could bring in his kingdom at any moment. Whoever acknowledges my mission will stand acknowledged before God at the judgment. But whoever denies it will be denied before God.

JOHN

Well, if we're that near the end what difference does it make what we do?

JESUS

We always stand before the end. That's what

gives our time its possibilities. You know
what the prophets of judgment say--when you
risk everything in the face of crisis you
actualize your inmost heart.

                    JOHN
             (looks at the others)
Have **you** ever heard a prophet say that? I know
things have gotten more serious lately, so
maybe I shouldn't say this. But I've got the
feeling he's taking another turn into one of
his strange periods. Teacher, we'd better slow
down and figure out what's going on.

                    JESUS
I know what's going on. This is where the road
north abruptly turns south.

                    10.

        Jesus and his disciples have returned to
Capernaum for a brief visit and are now on their way
out of town again. By the roadside on the edge of
town Jesus is talking to four or five disciples.

                    ANDREW
We're going all the way to Jerusalem? Isn't
that farther south than necessary?

                    JESUS
No, it's not too far.

                    PETER
But **why** are we going to Jerusalem? There's
plenty to do in Galilee; we've hardly touched
the crowds here.

                    JESUS
We're going because I haven't been, and I must
preach the kingdom of God in the holy city.
Besides, where else can a prophet die?

As Jesus and Peter are talking, a crowd of thirty or
forty people appears noisily on the scene with the
rest of the disciples.

                MAN IN THE CROWD
Teacher, I've brought my son to you because

he's got a dumb spirit, and often it seizes him
and dashes him down, and he foams at the mouth
and grinds his teeth and becomes rigid.   I
asked some of your disciples to cast it out,
but they couldn't do it.

                    JESUS
That's not the biggest surprise I've had in the
last eight months. Bring the boy to me.

Someone helps the father bring his son to Jesus.   In
Jesus' presence he is convulsed and rolls on the
ground foaming at the mouth.

                    JESUS
How long has he had this?

                    MAN
Since childhood.   And from time to time it's
cast him into the fire or into the water to
destroy him.   But if you can do anything, have
pity on us and help us.

                    JESUS
If I can.   All things are possible for one who
believes.

                    MAN
I believe....help my unbelief.

                    JESUS
You're an honest man.   We seem not to be
willing   enough   to   take   a   chance   on   the
mysterious power of God's goodness.   But then
God doesn't make it all that easy for us, does
he? He's present in the ordinary happenings of
our lives, there for us, just   beneath the
surface--but the surface is frequently dense.
(turning to the boy) You dumb and deaf spirit,
come out of him and never enter him again!

The boy is convulsed again and then lies there like a
corpse.

                    ANOTHER MAN
Is he dead?

Jesus takes the boy by the hand and raises him up.   He
and his father walk away.

70

JOHN

Teacher, there're some people here with children, and they want you to touch them, but we told them we were on our way to Jerusalem and had to get moving.

JESUS

We're not in that big a hurry. Let the children come to me and don't prevent them, for to such belongs the kingdom of God. In fact, I tell you that if you don't accept the kingdom like a little child, you won't enter it.

Several parents bring their children up to Jesus, and, sitting on a rock, he takes one of them on his lap.

JOHN

I thought you'd been telling us to grow up and leave home. Now we're supposed to return to childhood. What childish thing are we supposed to do?

JESUS

No particular childish thing--but something much more far reaching. If an adult becomes a child, he makes a new beginning, starts all over again with nothing--but God.

During this exchange a well dressed man has been pushing through the crowd to Jesus.

MAN

Good teacher, what must I do to enter the kingdom and inherit eternal life?

JESUS

Why do you call me good? No one is good but God. But you know the commandments: Do not kill, do not commit adultery, do not steal, do not bear false witness, do not defraud, honor your father and mother.

MAN

Teacher, I've observed all these things from my youth.

JESUS

My friend, you're aware of where you are.

71

You've done all these things, but you've sensed
you may not have eternal life. Otherwise why
would you have asked the way? You think you
may not quite have it--and you're right. You
lack one thing--go sell all you have and give
the proceeds to the poor. Then you'll have
treasure in heaven--and come follow me.

The man looks at Jesus intently and then, dropping his
head, walks away. Jesus watches him go and then turns
back to the disciples and the others.

                    JESUS
It's very hard for a rich man to start over
with nothing. It is in fact easier for a camel
to go through the eye of a needle than for a
rich man to enter the kingdom of God.

                    PETER
Well, god, what hope does any of us have for
salvation? Even the worst of us has something.
Who can be saved?

                    JESUS
It's impossible with man. But all things are
possible with God--even freeing us from ourselves.

                    PETER
Actually, we really have given up everything to
follow you.

                    JESUS
You're very likely going to have a chance to
prove that, Peter.

                    11.

     Jesus and his disciples are now in Jerusalem, and
he has just led them into the temple's Court of
Gentiles. It is a busy, noisy, bustling place where
merchants are selling animals for sacrifice along with
the necessary wine, oil, and salt; and money-changers
are available to exchange the Roman and Greek coins of
Jewish pilgrims for the Jewish coinage required for
paying the annual half-sheckel temple tax.

                    PETER
What are we going to do here?

                    72

                    JESUS
We're going to turn this place inside out.

                    JAMES
Why?

                    JESUS
As an act of protest.

                    PETER
Against what?

                    JESUS
Against turning the gentile's place of worship
into a market place. God has said his temple
is to be a house of prayer for all nations.
And against religious leaders who put wealth
and power, yes, and even obedience to the law,
or some parts of it, above how an ordinary,
poor sinful Jew stands before God or whether he
has bread to eat. The business transacted here
is worth a fortune you know. So let's get to
it.

Jesus begins turning over the tables of the money-
changers and pushing the merchants out. The disciples
fall to, following his example, with considerable
enthusiasm. Other people in the area stop and look on
in amazement. In a few moments a group of priests
along with Asa, the scribe, and some temple guards
appear angrily on the scene.

                    PRIEST
               (to Jesus)
What do you think you're doing?

                    ASA
He's continuing what he's been doing. I've
told you. This is what it's led to.

                    JESUS
I'm acting against wickedness.

                    PRIEST
You're protesting wickedness? You! You're
destroying the worship of God. You're worse
than a Samaritan, and we're going to get you.
(shouting) Seize him, guards!

As the guards apprehend Jesus a band of Roman soldiers, led by a centurion, appears to check the situation.

                    CENTURION
    What's going on here?

                    PRIEST
    This man is rebelling against God--and Rome-- disrupting the city.

                    CENTURION
    It doesn't appear that anyone has been killed, or even injured!

                    PRIEST
    We stopped him just in time.

                    CENTURION
    There're always flare-ups at Passover time. I don't think it's serious--let him go.

The guards reluctantly release Jesus.

                    PRIEST
                (to Jesus)
    We'll destroy you.

Jesus is walking away with his disciples.

                    JESUS
                (to the disciples)
    Passover is in a few days, and I've arranged a room for us to eat the meal in. John, will you and James make the preparations?

                    12.

    The chief priests, elders, and scribes are gathered in the palace of Caiaphas, the high priest.

                    CAIAPHAS
    Something must be done about this Jesus from Galilee.

                    PRIEST
    Let's kill him secretly before the Passover. If we wait until after the Feast begins, his followers may rise up.

SECOND PRIEST

I don't think we can succeed at that. There are too many around now who seem to believe in him. And the Romans are very vigilant at festival time.

CAIAPHAS

Yes, I think we have to bring the Romans in on it.

PRIEST

They didn't seem too interested the other day.

CAIAPHAS

They can be made interested.

PRIEST

We could say he tried to destroy the temple.

SECOND PRIEST

As you yourself said, the Romans didn't seem too disturbed by that escapade. But some of his followers evidently believe he's the Messiah--or the Christ as our Greek-speaking brothers would put it. As a matter of fact, in disrupting the temple business he was attacking us, and we have our authority from Rome. He is seditious. The most effective plan will simply be to tell the Romans he thinks he's the Messiah, the king of the Jews.

CAIAPHAS

Simplicity is the soul of wisdom. I'll take care of it.

13.

On the Thursday evening beginning 15 Nisan Jesus and his disciples are in a large upper room reclining on cushions around a table, ready to eat the Passover.

JESUS

My brothers, my friends, I think I will not be with you many days more, for the opposing forces are ready to act. I have some things to say to you, some things to share with you-- including my fears. I'm afraid you're going to abandon me, for it is written in Scripture--I will strike the shepherd and the sheep will be scattered.

They all protest that they will not forsake him.

                    PETER
Even if every one of them falls away, I never will.

                    JESUS
Peter, before the cock crows you'll deny me three times.

                    PETER
               (with vehemence)
If I must die with you, I will not deny you.

                    JESUS
I hope that's true. But be it as it may, I believe I'll be vindicated soon, and you'll share that vindication. That's what we're here for tonight. In these last months I've taken many things on myself, so I'll take one more-- to change the Passover ritual which for countless generations has sustained our life. I offer you bread and wine, the ordinary bread and wine we've shared so many times. Now it represents all that has happened among us and will happen in these next hours. From now on when you eat the flesh of the grain and drink the blood of the grape, nature and history and our own fragile lives come together, and I will be present with you till the kingdom of God comes.

Jesus passes the bread and wine around the table, and they all eat and drink silently and solemnly. Jesus notices a look of distress and questioning on the face of one disciple.

                    JESUS
Bartholomew, what's bothering you?

                    BARTHOLOMEW
Is this all we're going to have?

                    JESUS
It's a lot, but it's not all. I have one more parable to leave with you.

JAMES

A parable?

JESUS

A parable. The prophet Daniel has told us that one like a Son of Man will come on the clouds with power and glory and marvelous light. This is the one who will show that I've preached God's word and done his truth. He'll sit on a glorious throne and gather all mankind before him. He will divide them into two groups, the sheep and the goats, the sheep on his right and the goats on his left. Then he will say to the sheep, "Come, O blessed of my Father, and inherit the kingdom prepared for you from the foundation of the world. For I was hungry and you gave me food, I was thirsty and you gave me drink, I was a stranger and you welcomed me, I was naked and you clothed me, I was sick and you visited me, I was in prison and you came to me."

BARTHOLOMEW

But the Son of Man comes in the future--if he comes. I thought all of this was supposed to be for now.

JESUS

It is for now. The sheep will answer the Son of Man, "Lord, when did we see you hungry and feed you or thirsty and give you a drink? When did we see you naked and clothe you or sick or in prison and visit you?" And the Son of Man will answer them, "Truly I say to you, inasmuch as you did it for one of my brothers or sisters you did it for me."

BARTHOLOMEW

When a sheep--I mean a person--visits a prisoner, he visits the Son of Man?

JESUS

The Son of Man comes before he comes. Watch for him.

BARTHOLOMEW

What about the goats?

JESUS

I think you can figure that out....It's getting
late. I want to get out of the city and go to
the Mount of Olives.

They all get up and leave.

14.

Having arrived at the Garden of Gethsemane, Jesus
and the disciples enter.

JESUS
(to the disciples)
Will you sit here and watch a while? I'm going
farther into the garden to pray.

He walks away from them to be alone and drops to his
knees. They promptly fall asleep.

JESUS

God, my Father, I have known a call from you to
a mission, and I have lived in the world with
people. Life has taken hold of me, and I do
not wish to leave it. But it seems that I'm
going to, so on the eve of my leave-taking, let
me remember some things with joy and longing.
Let me remember before you--before you--Father
in heaven, what has touched me in this world.
I remember still the softness of Chara's hair
and the warmth of her skin, the light in her
face when she speaks of love. I remember,
Father, the sense of oneness with you when I
have proclaimed your kingdom and your forgiveness, the look of shocked recognition in the
eyes of my alien and guilty brothers and
sisters who see that they are the ones who are
loved. I remember the stars in the black sky
over Syria....and the last of the winter rains
rushing down the river-beds into the green
Galilean springtime. I remember eating and
drinking at a wedding. I do not want to
die....I do not want to die. Is there another
way? What does this have to do with eating and
drinking at a wedding?.... No, Father, there's
no other way. If I must die for the sake of
letting others know that you are near to them
regardless of where they are, then I will
die....Now   I   know   what   time   it   is.

Jesus gets up and walks back to where the disciples are, finding them asleep.

                        JESUS
                   (to himself)
     My time is here, and they're asleep.   There
     must be a parable in that.

Just as Jesus finishes these words a large group arrives--composed of temple police, sent by the chief priests and scribes, and a band of Roman soldiers. The centurion who had intervened in the temple is in charge of the whole group.

                      CENTURION
     Jesus of Nazareth, I hereby place you under
     arrest.

                        JESUS
     You! Why you, why Rome? I expected the temple
     police but not you.   Why only days ago you
     saved my life in the temple.

                      CENTURION
     Well...now I've got to arrest you.

                        JESUS
     But why? My mission has **not** been political.

                      CENTURION
     The governor will make the charges known to you
     (to his men). Bind his hands.

The soldiers seize Jesus and tie his hands.   The disciples flee from the scene, and the officers take Jesus away at spear point.

                        15.

     Jesus has been imprisoned in the Praetorium. Early in the morning while it is still dark Peter comes back into the city stealthily and enters a courtyard near the Praetorium where several people are warming themselves around a fire.   Hesitantly Peter joins them.

                 HIGH PRIEST'S MAID
                   (to Peter)
     Who are you? Oh, I know. You were with the
     Nazarene.

                    PETER
I don't understand what you're talking about.

                    MAID
              (to the others)
But he is one of them. Obviously he's a
Galilean. Listen to his accent.

                    PETER
God almighty, do you think everybody from
Galilee is following him?

                   BYSTANDER
I know you're one of them. I saw you in the
temple with him when he was tearing the place
up.

                    PETER
Jesus Christ, what do I have to say to convince
you I'm not his disciple?

The cock crows.

ACT III

Jerusalem

An Answer--A Question

Not long after daybreak the same morning Pilate, the governor, sits on the judgment seat which has been placed on a platform in the courtyard of the Praetorium. Jesus stands before Pilate--along with a delegation of priests and a small band of soldiers led by the centurion, who have brought Jesus before the governor. Below the platform, looking on and eagerly waiting for something to begin, is a large crowd, among whom several of Jesus' disciples are trying to hide themselves.

                    PILATE
So, Centurion, this is the king of the Jews you've brought me so early in the morning.

                    CENTURION
He's been charged with claiming that title.

                    PILATE
               (to Jesus)
Are you the king of the Jews?

Jesus says nothing but looks intently at Pilate. The priests are getting edgy and one speaks.

                    PRIEST
Of course, he's the king of the Jews. That is, he's falsely claimed to be. He's stirred up the nation and perverted our people--and he's even forbidden paying taxes to Caesar.

                    PILATE
               (to Jesus)
Are you such a king?

Jesus still refuses to answer. Two of his disciples in the crowd whisper loudly to each other.

                    JOHN
I thought maybe he was the Messiah, or at least a great prophet. But he won't say anything.

                    JAMES
Let's hope the fishing is still there in Galilee. I don't think we can believe he's the Messiah.

PILATE

He's not acting much like a king right now.
He's certainly silent enough. Why don't I
release him? After all, it's Passover time.

PRIEST

Release Barabbas for us, not the Galilean.

PILATE

You mean you want me to release Barabbas the
murderer? And what shall I do with your king?

PRIEST

Crucify him!

The priests motion urgently and impatiently to the
crowd.

CROWD
(with a roar)
Crucify him! Crucify him!

JOHN
(to James)
I don't think we can believe anything in this
world.

PILATE
(to Jesus)
I'm going to ask you one more time. Are you
the king of the Jews?

JESUS

Of course...of course, I'm king of the Jews.
Haven't you ever seen my army? I have an army
of twelve men. The only reason they aren't
here now is they're out gathering new recruits.

PILATE

Well, at least we're getting something to go on
now. Tell me--your majesty, where does that
put Caesar? Do you in fact forbid your subjects to pay taxes to Caesar?

JESUS

No, I don't forbid it. What I tell them is--
render to Caesar the things that are Caesar's
and to God the things that are God's.

PILATE
And what exactly is Caesar's?

JESUS
A good question--your excellency, a good question. What is Caesar's? Nothing, absolutely
nothing--except--what God gives him, for a
brief season, and for his--that is, God's--
purpose--your excellency.

PILATE
I'm beginning not to like you--your majesty.
But let me ask you--how is Caesar to carry out
the purpose of the God of the Jews?

JESUS
Whoever would be first must be last. Whoever
would be great must be servant of all.

PILATE
You call that a guide for practical politics?

JESUS
It does seem I've drifted into politics,
doesn't it--your excellency? No, not a guide--
but a limit, at least.

PILATE
And do you think Tiberius Caesar has ruled
within your limits?

JESUS
I have observed that the kings of the nations
lord it over their subjects.... They are not
to.

PILATE
And what **are** they to do?

JESUS
They are to wash the feet of dusty travelers.

PILATE
Let me assure you, by god, that Tiberius
Caesar, and his deputies, can lord it over
whomsoever they choose. Centurion, take him
out and crucify him.

The soldiers rough Jesus up and lead him away.

2.

On a hill outside of Jerusalem three men are hanging on crosses. Jesus is the one in the middle, and he has been there for some hours. The same centurion is there with soldiers who, having nailed Jesus to the cross, are now keeping order. They allow people to wander by and mill around the foot of the cross. The centurion watches everything carefully. A soldier who has been on a brief mission returns to the group and speaks.

SOLDIER

How's the king?

SECOND SOLDIER

Not too good. He seems to be weakening.

SOLDIER

Well, let's try to pump him up a little, say something encouraging to him.

SECOND SOLDIER

Here's a cheer for him--All hail the power of Jesus' name!

ALL THE SOLDIERS

All hail the power of Jesus' name!

SOLDIER

Now let's call him names. You know, juice him up by calling him famous names.

SECOND SOLDIER

Here's one--Alexander the Great.

SOLDIER

That's a good one. All together now.

He gives them a mock serious signal with his hand.

ALL THE SOLDIERS

Alexander the Great!

SOLDIER

That's wonderful. We've had one for Greece,

86

now let's have one for Rome.   What about Julius
Caesar?

SOLDIERS
Yeah!

SOLDIER
All together now.

He gives them another signal and leads their acclama-
tion.

SOLDIERS
Julius Caesar!   Hail Caesar!

THIRD SOLDIER
The man's suffering.   Let's give him some wine
to ease his pain.

SOLDIER
Why not?   It would help relieve the boredom.

They soak a sponge in wine, put it on the end of a
reed and hold it up to Jesus' mouth.   He shakes his
head exhaustedly, refusing it.   While this is going on
three or four disciples are talking on the edge of the
crowd.

ANDREW
Listen to how they're talking to him.

JAMES
If God was with him, they couldn't ridicule him
like that.

JOHN
He   couldn't   possibly   be   the   Messiah....And
whatever became of the kingdom of God?

JAMES
And the Son of Man hasn't showed up.   I thought
he was supposed to vindicate him.

BARTHOLOMEW
What was that he said about the Son of Man
being poor, or naked, or a prisoner?

As the disciples have been talking, several priests
have   walked   up   near   the   foot   of   the   cross.

PRIEST

Hey, Christ, you up there on the cross--how did
you ever get exalted to such a high position?
You're so far away up there we can hardly see
you.

SECOND PRIEST

Yes, Christ, we can hardly tell who you are.

THIRD PRIEST

Why don't you come down and bless us poor
mortals?

PRIEST

Yes, Christ, come down to us, or rise up, or
make some kind of move that we can see and
believe in you.

The disciples are still on one extreme edge of the
crowd.

JOHN

He couldn't possibly be the Messiah of God.

JESUS

My God, my God, why have you forsaken me?

Jesus' head falls limp as the centurion who is still
on the edge of the crowd at the other extreme watches
intently.

CENTURION

Truly this man was the Son of God.

3.

A very few days later the disciples are gathered
in the same room in Jerusalem in which they ate their
last meal with Jesus. They are sitting around on the
floor talking.

ANDREW

Why are we still sitting around here anyway?

JAMES

Because there's nothing left to do.

PETER

There is something to do.

                                        JOHN
What?

                                        PETER
Waiting. Waiting is something to do.

                                        JOHN
Waiting for what? If I'm going to sit around
waiting, I've got to know what I'm waiting for.

                                        PETER
I don't know exactly. Maybe we're waiting for
the shame to wear off. I denied I ever knew him
you know.

                                        JOHN
Don't remind me, I know. The rest of us didn't
do any better.

                                        JAMES
Could we have? He said the kingdom was coming
soon--immediately, but it didn't come. So why
should we feel that guilty, and what is there
to wait for?

                                        PETER
We're guilty all right. But maybe the kingdom
will come, in some kind of surprising way. He
said God comes for sinners.

                                        ANDREW
Then he'll probably come for us. You know he
reminded us that seed has a hard time coming to
harvest--but it comes.

                                        PETER
Yes, and there was that parable about the
farmer who sows and then doesn't have to do
anything until the harvest comes. The earth
makes the seed grow and we have time to wait
around in.

                                        JAMES
Well, if you want to go back to parables there
was the one about the doorkeeper. Waiting
doesn't seem all that easy. The doorkeeper has
always got to be on the watch because he
doesn't know when the master is coming back
home.

                                         89

                        PETER
Maybe Jesus is going to come back.

                        JOHN
Come back? How could he possibly?

                        PETER
He used to say God would vindicate him and he'd
quote Hosea to us--after two days he will
revive us, on the third day he will raise us
up.

                        JOHN
But even if he expected it, how could it be?
Are you talking about rising from the dead?
That doesn't come until the end of the world,
when God brings his kingdom and makes
everything new, when he creates the world
again.

                        ANDREW
Jesus did do new things.

                        JOHN
And he got a lot out of it.

                        ANDREW
Well maybe if he doesn't come back the Son of
Man will come.

                        BARTHOLOMEW
Maybe he's already come. Remember the teacher
said he comes before he comes.

                        JAMES
He hasn't come. The Son of Man will come on
the clouds with the angels in great light. How
could we miss that?

                        PETER
We've missed a few things.

                        JAMES
But you couldn't miss that.

                        JOHN
I'm sure we missed a lot. I know something
important has happened, at least I think it

has. But I can't get hold of what it is.
Let's go back to our fishing. It's still
there.

                    PETER
No, we're waiting. Let's wait a little longer.

                    JAMES
I think you really believe he's going to
appear. What would he look like if he rose
from the dead?

                    ANDREW
He'd be like a spirit.

                    JAMES
Can you see a spirit?

                    PETER
Maybe so. They're like light.

                    ANDREW
Whatever. He'd be able to walk through that
door without even opening it, or just come
through the wall.

                    JOHN
What's the point of coming back from the dead
if you don't have a body?

                    JAMES
Yes, that's right. If he came back, he'd have
a body.

                    JOHN
Sure he would. You could touch him, just like
anybody else.

                    PETER
He'd probably want something to eat.

                    JAMES
I've never known him to turn down a good meal.

                    JOHN
Or a cup of wine.

                    PETER
I can hardly believe it's only been a few days

since he shared bread and wine with us--in this room. He said the meal represents him and when we eat bread and drink wine he would be with us.

                    JOHN
Where is he?

                    PETER
We're waiting.

                    JAMES
Do you remember that crazy wedding feast in Nazareth?

                    ANDREW
Do I ever? The teacher was having a wonderful time--we all were.

                    JAMES
He sent us out for more wine.

                    PETER
And he was telling everybody to be happy.

                    ANDREW
Which everyone was pretty much doing.

                    JOHN
When the host got mad and threw us all out.

They all laugh loudly.

                    JAMES
I'm hungry right now. Let's pass around the food.

They distribute bread and wine to each other and begin to eat and continue to talk.

                    PETER
Levi, do you remember that dinner at your house the day you joined us?

                    LEVI
I'll never forget it.

                    ANDREW
We were eating away when Asa and a few friends

came in—and Asa said, "Why does he eat with tax collectors and sinners?"

                    JAMES
Do you remember what the teacher said?

                    PETER
Of course, I can hear him now just as if he was with us—"because I'm hungry, I eat with them because I'm hungry."

                    JOHN
But why with these sinners, Jesus, why these sinners?

                    PETER
Because they're sick and need a physician.

                    JOHN
Well, their appetites are certainly healthy enough.

                    PETER
But their hearts, Asa, their hearts. I have something to share with them.

                    JOHN
Then why not share it with the righteous? What good is the law, Jesus, if obedience doesn't deserve something?

                    PETER
That's what we're trying to find out, Asa. That's what we're trying to find out.

They suddenly stop talking and look at each other in startled fashion, not quite understanding what is happening.

                    ANDREW
There's one parable he told more often than any other.

                    JAMES
The one about the boy who left home and abandoned his family.

                    PETER
And wasted everything that had been given him and turned himself into a gentile sinner.

ANDREW

And then he returned home hoping his father
would take him back as a servant.

JAMES

But his father came running out, running out,
can you believe that? And he embraced him and
received him back with a ring and shoes.

ANDREW

And he called for a feast and he said, "My son
who was lost is found, my son who was dead is
alive."

JOHN

Peter, when Jesus was telling that story did
you ever feel that God receives us--the way
that father received his son?.....But that was
long ago, and much has happened. Could God
ever forgive us for leaving him in the night
and letting him die?

PETER

When we eat the bread and drink the wine.....we
are forgiven.

4.

On a warm, bright afternoon in October of about
1970 an American couple with their two young sons are
sitting in an outdoor restaurant in Vienna's Kärntner
Strasse. Across the street from them a misshapen
beggar is sitting on the sidewalk in front of an ele-
gant store. The family is eating and talking.

JOY

Bart, I think you could sit here all afternoon
absorbing the glow of Vienna.

BART

I could, Joy, I really could. I simply do not
know when a city has so enchanted me. Last
night when the four of us were walking down
Kärntner Strasse to the opera I had the strange
feeling that everything was very familiar. We
looked right, we were in the right place.

JOY

You almost sound as if in this whole thing we
were on the stage rather than watching it.

                    BART
There is something a little theatrical about
it, I'll admit it.

Bart glances across the street, as he continues to do
from time to time as they talk.

                    BART (cont.)
It's all just too glamorous--for a boy from
North Carolina. This street is too beautiful--
these stores, the things in them, the lights in
the windows, the lights sparkling in the silver
buttons of our blazers last night, the people
walking up and down this street. That October
sun is absolute gold (smiles playfully). Did
you notice how it reflects off the nylons on
those beautiful legs that just passed.

                    MARK
Watch it, Dad.

                    PAUL
He is watching it.   Has he ever missed
something like that? (all laughing)

                    JOY
          (with good humored self-
           confidence)
You're a wicked man, Bart.

                    BART
Not seriously wicked, not in that regard
anyway.

                    JOY
But you are a hopeless romantic.

                    BART
I hope not hopeless, but I am a romantic. I'm
romantic about us, and I'm romantic about
Europe. You've heard me talk about it enough
times before. I've often suspected that the
most civilized time and place to live was
Europe between 1870 and 1914. And Vienna was
the refined, distilled essence of it.

                    JOY
Now you are getting hopeless.

                     95

                    BART
No, not really. I know very well that behind
all that music and dancing, and drinking new
wine in Grinzing, and while all those bourgeois
ladies were composing their lives on Freud's
couch, the government was moving, if not
racing, from one crisis to another.

                    JOY
Bart, why do you keep looking across the
street? Is something distracting you from all
of this Viennese drama?

                    BART
There is something very disruptive and perplex-
ing in the drama.   If the play was ever a
comedy, it has become a very serious one.

                    PAUL
How is that?

                    BART
Do you see that beggar over there? (nodding his
head in the direction of the other side of the
street).   That poor, misshapen man sitting in
front of that shop--that very fashionable shop.
There's a bowl beside him on the sidewalk, and
he's begging for money. He can't talk. The
way he looks does the asking. Yesterday when I
was walking by myself I noticed him--I noticed
his poverty in the midst of all this wealth.
People were walking by and putting in coins. I
put in a couple of bills, and he saw it.   I
didn't give him much, but he saw it was more
than he usually got, and this unbelievable
smile lighted up his face. Light was literally
radiating. I wondered if the sun was shining
on him at a strange angle.   But the light
shining in that face came from inside of him,
from some source I couldn't see. The dispro-
portion between the almost nothing I gave him
and the totality of his gratitude is an
incongruity my imagination can hardly get hold
of.   I gave him so little, but he received so
much.   I can't make it fit, I can not understand it, but I will never forget the light.

                    JOY
It really did move you, you hadn't told me.

                    96

                        BART
This is the first time I could even begin to
talk about it.

                        JOY
What will you do about it?

                        BART
I'll always remember it, but what will I do
about it? That question makes me a little
uneasy, and sad. Perhaps I'll let all these
other lights overcome that one and force it
down into some dark corner of my heart.
Remember Pascal's infinite abyss that we can't
fill no matter how hard we try. Maybe that's
where the light is going to be pushed.

                        JOY
Then perhaps it will illumine the infinite
abyss.

                        BART
                 (smiling)
I don't call you Joy for nothing.

                        MARK
What time is it, Dad?

                        BART
It's time to see the world by that light.

                        PAUL
No, Dad, what time is it?

                        BART
It's time to go back to the hotel and get
dressed for dinner and the opera.

                        MARK
Dad.....I mean, what **time** is it?

                        BART
                 (looking at his watch)
It's four-thirty in the afternoon.

                        JOY
What about the light?

                         BART
I have to pay attention to it.

                         JOY
How will you?

                         BART
I don't know, less well than I should. But it
won't go out.

                         JOY
And in the meantime?

                         BART
In the meantime--we should not let the meantime
last too long. (smiles) But there's time for
another slice of bread.

                         JOY
And a glass of Vienna wine.

They pass the bread around the table.